St Macarius Press

2020 Second Edition amended with a richer collection of sayings

First edition © 2019 St Macarius Press
Monastery of Saint Macarius the Great
(Egypt)
P.O. BOX 2780
Cairo - Egypt
E-mail: info@stmacariuspress.com
Phone: +201282211923

Our Address in the USA:
13303 Scotch Run Ct
Centreville, VA 20120-6428
United States of America

ALL RIGHTS RESERVED.
No part of this publication may be reproduced, stored in a retrieval system, or transmitted in any form or by any means—electronic, mechanical, graphic, photocopy, recording, taping, information storage, or any other—without written permission of the publisher.

ANBA EPIPHANIUS
BISHOP AND ABBOT
OF THE MONASTERY OF SAINT MACARIUS THE GREAT
(EGYPT)

SO GREAT A SALVATION

BIBLICAL MEDITATIONS OF A CONTEMPORARY DESERT FATHER

*IN APPENDIX,
ANBA EPIPHANIUS' APOPHTHEGMS*

FOREWORD BY H.H. POPE TAWADROS II

*EDITION AND TRANSLATION FROM ARABIC BY
SAMUEL KALDAS & RAMZA BASSILIOUS*

*PREFACE BY
MONK WADID EL MACARI*

*INTRODUCTION BY
MONK MARKOS EL MAKARI*

ST MACARIUS PRESS
MONASTERY OF SAINT MACARIUS THE GREAT (EGYPT)

Mafāhīm 'inğīliyya
Original Title

978-1-7329852-8-5
ISBN

2020939736
Library of Congress Control Number

Biblica
Series

H.H. Pope Tawadros II
Foreword

Wadid el Macari
Preface

Markos el Makari
Introduction

Samuel Kaldas and Ramza Bassilious
Edition and Translation from Arabic

David Georgy
Cover

5" x 8"
Format

301
Pages

ON THE COVER: Picture taken of Anba Epiphanius in the Primatial Abbey of Saint Anselm on the Aventine (Rome - Italy) on September 15th 2016

CONTENTS

Abbreviations	7
Foreword by H. H. Pope Tawadros II	9
Preface	17
Introduction	33
Some Significant Dates	57
The Fullness of Time	61
A Branch From the Root of Jesse	71
Christ the Firstborn	81
Christ the Light of the World	93
The Pure in Heart	105
Children of Abraham	117
Seek the Lord	129
The Transfiguration of Christ and the Tranfiguration of the Disciples	137
Hosanna to the Son of David	145
Give to Caesar what is Caesar's and to God what is God's	155
The Bronze Serpent	165
The Lord Jesus Was Crucified For My Sake	177
True Joy Springs Out of the Empty Tomb	187

The Gifts of the Holy Spirit	199
Children of God	209
Spiritual Understanding of Physical Training in the Letters of St Paul	219
Trials as the Expression of God's Love	229
Our Life in Christ	239
Gain and Loss in St Paul's Profitable Business	251
Coals of Fire	261
Christ's Triumphal Procession	271
The Last Trumpet	281
Appendix: Some Apophthegms of Our Father Bishop Anba Epiphanius	293

ABBREVIATIONS

ANF Alexander Roberts, James Donaldson et al. (eds.), *Ante-Nicene Fathers*, Vols. I-X, (Buffalo: NY, Christian Literature Publishing Co., 1885-1896).

Bustān Anba Epiphanius (ed.), *Bustān al-Ruhbān*, (Wādī al-Naṭrūn: Monastery of Saint Macarius the Great, 2013).

GELNT Walter Bauer, *A Greek-English Lexicon of the New Testament and Other Early Christian Literature*, (Chicago, IL: University of Chicago Press, 2001).

Mishnah Herbert Danby (ed.), *The Mishnah*, (Oxford: Oxford University Press, 1933).

NPNF Philip Schaff et al. (eds.), *Nicene and Post-Nicene Fathers*, series 2, Vols. I-XIV, (Buffalo: NY, Christian Literature Publishing Co., 1886-1900).

PG	J.-P. Migne (ed.), *Patrologiae cursus completus. Series graeca,* (Paris-Turnhout, 1857-1866).
SC	*Sources Chrétiennes*, (Paris 1942 ss.).
TDNT	Gerhard Kittel, Gerhard Friedrich et al. (eds.), *Theological Dictionary of the New Testament*, vols. I-X, (Grand Rapids, MI: William B. Eerdmans Publishing Company, 1977).
Ward	Benedicta Ward (ed.), *The Sayings of the Desert Fathers* (Kalamazoo, MI: Cistercians Publications, 1984).

FOREWORD

BY H.H. TAWADROS II

Anba Epiphanius was a bishop who illuminated and brightened all those who knew him. Despite the pain that has gripped us all, and myself in particular, we entrust him to the hope of the resurrection, as our Orthodox Church teaches us to do when we take leave of our loved ones.

In the face of this terrible event, our faith in God the Pantocrator is not shaken. It is God, in fact, who sustains this life. Nothing escapes Him, nothing and no one. We believe, rather, we indeed live at the height and in the depth of this faith, that God rules our lives in their smallest details. He is in control of our birth and also of our departure from this life.

We also believe that He is the Benefactor par excellence. God does good in every moment and in every morning. He does good to all, to the good and the bad, and makes His sun rise on the righteous and on the wicked, on the saints and on sinners. Finally, we believe that He is the Lover of Mankind. Sinners are loved by Him. He loves every human being. Even if He does not love sin, He loves the human being and hopes that he or she will repent. He loves the sinner and hopes he will repent; He hopes he will wake up before it is too late.

In Anba Epiphanius, this beloved brother of ours who has left us very suddenly, we beheld a radiant example, a luminous star by whose light the whole world was illuminated. A luminous star that shone in every place he went or he served in. We learn many things from his life. Allow me to speak of three particular qualities: meekness of wisdom, great culture, simplicity of life.

WISE MEEKNESS

He was endowed with the meekness of wisdom. Anyone who saw him or spoke with him, immediately sensed this powerful, sincere mildness which encompassed his entire life. He was meek even in his silence, in his gentle smile, in expressing his right opinions, always seeking integrity. He always sought the peace of the Church, along with that of the monastery and of all those around him. This was not meekness alone, but meekness adorned also with wisdom.

Whenever he engaged in discussion, he did it with a wisdom given to him by long experience, as well the grace of God. When I asked him to participate in meetings or sit on a committee, he was wise even in choosing the committees, choosing the members, choosing what they would discuss, whether he was present or not. His views were always insightful.

I must confess that I often consulted him before making my decisions. The meekness of wisdom, brothers and sisters, is a rare quality at this time. Perhaps we sometimes encounter meekness but a meekness that lacks wisdom.

I did not know him before the fathers of this thriving monastery, the elders and the monks, elected him to be a bishop, in February 2013. He and one other monk attained the highest number of votes, and the monastery was very happy with him; perhaps you all remember this too, and my fathers the bishops: the day of his enthronement, how joyful that day was.

GREAT CULTURE

Anba Epiphanius had a remarkable cultural calibre and was a great scholar. This is a fitting description of him; his learning was not superficial, in all his lectures, his studies and his research, in the manuscripts he investigated, he was deeply knowledgeable.

I often asked him to attend international conferences as the official representative of the Coptic Orthodox Church, the face of the Church of Egypt; a shining face that truly illumined the world with his knowledge. These are not merely words of praise, but the reality.

He was abundant in knowledge; when he participated and gave lectures at the seminars we held for the monks and nuns, they learned a great deal from him, asked him all sorts of questions, and he put his knowledge at the disposal of all.

To be a bishop, my beloved brothers and sisters, is not simply a name or a title, nor a cassock or an external appearance. Our beloved brother was truly an example and a model, who occupied his position before the Churches of the world bringing honour to the Coptic Church.

His abundant knowledge produced a number of books published by the monastery: various books on many subjects, for instance, liturgical studies on the Liturgy of St Cyril, or in the field of Biblical studies, such as on the book of Genesis—I am not giving a complete list but only a few examples—or manuscripts which he succeeded in investigating.

When I visited this monastery on March 10th 2014, a full year after his ordination, I spent a day there in the company *of the beloved fathers which I remember very fondly; we prayed together and praised together. Bishop Epiphanius was present with us, and presented six monks to be ordained as priests. I visited this flourishing monastery with the fathers and its library of manuscripts, along with all its other sacred places; we are proud to have this monastery as one of our Coptic monasteries.*

He was abundant in knowledge; rarely do we encounter such a father.

SIMPLICITY OF LIFE

The third thing is that, although he had the meekness of wisdom and although he was abundant in knowledge, he lived a very simple life. His cell, his way of dressing, and his food bear witness to this. He lived very simply; even when he attended conferences in Egypt and abroad, he always took the lowest place (cf. Lk. 14:10).

He was even simple in his teaching: he did not use sophisticated concepts or terms, or words that might cause his hearers not to understand. When he responded to questions from the youth or from the fathers on various occasions, he chose simple and accessible answers. To answer simply is depth, for it allows the person to understand and learn and be satisfied.

We have indeed lost Anba Epiphanius, but—just as his name is derived from 'light'—he was a light in the midst of our Holy Synod. His image, his example and his name will remain eternal.

Blessed is the Monastery of St Macarius which brought forth this blessed person; blessed is this ancient monastery, in which saints have lived and travelled the spiritual path, and glorified God in their lives, leading holy lives recorded in the annals of history. Therefore, blessed is this monastery, which brought forth a bishop such as this, through whom the world was illuminated.

I testify before God and before you that Anba Epiphanius was a shining example of learning and spiritual life and spiritual stature. He graduated from medical school; in his work as a doctor, and as a student before that, he was a remarkable person, always peaceable. His family connected him to the Church from his earliest years.

In his thirtieth year, he entered the monastery and was discipled by the elder fathers, loved them and was loved by them. After nearly thirty years in the monastery, its beloved fathers elected him to the episcopacy; he became a bishop and a member of the Holy Synod of our Church.

Although his episcopacy lasted no more than five years and a few months, he presented us with a living message: 'What is your life? For what is your life? It is even a vapor that appears for a little time and then vanishes away' (Jas 4:14). This is life.

If we are not comforted and instructed by this man of angelic character, gifted to us by heaven as a shining lamp—if we do not learn and draw comfort and let him be our example, we will lose a great deal. He dwelt among us as a bishop. Of course, he brought this same beautiful character to the Monastery of St Macarius, but when he became a bishop, he brought it to the whole church. He travelled much, and everywhere he went, grace, blessing, joy, spirituality and true monasticism went with him.

Monasticism, my beloved brethren, is a spiritual establishment, and it ought to be dazzlingly bright; this is our responsibility, all of us: that monasticism should be a shining example. The grievous blow that has befallen us concerns the entire world. International and state bodies have offered us their condolences, along with the International Council of Churches *and the* Pro Oriente Foundation, *regional Christian councils and the Churches here in Egypt and various organisations, each in their capacity, have expressed their condolences by their presence and by their words.*

His departure is a great blow, and has struck our Church and monastery to no small degree. But as I said at the beginning, we have faith in God the Pantocrator.

Blessed are you, blessed bishop, blessed are you who have lived among us offering us a splendid example and a luminous presence. Even though you were among us only for a short while, we have learned much from you. You have been a message from heaven, manifest to all of us.

Please, brothers and sisters, learn from this man's life. Learn from his writings and from his character. Truly, he has been taken from us, and has become as a shining jewel set in a place of honour.

Now he is in heaven, where is the presence of God and the fellowship of the saints and the just, and heavenly joy, heavenly peace, a place far removed from all earthly cares, hardships and ambitions.

O man, what will you reap? Will you reap dust? Whatever you acquire, whatever thoughts and desires you set your mind upon, what will you reap? In the end, it will be nothing but the dust of the earth.

For this reason, this blessed bishop has presented us with a perfect homily, teaching us that life can end in an instant.

Let us repent, my brethren. Let us repent truly. For when we stand before God, we will be unable to say anything to

Him except through our repentance. Our beloved brother called us to this, as we bid him farewell. He has departed, it is true, but he lives in our hearts, for those we love do not die, but live in our hearts. He lives in the memory of the Church, in the memory of the monastery, and in the memories of those beloved people who interacted with him. He lives and has begun to intercede for us, praying for our weakness and our pains. He prays for us in heaven, remembering this monastery which trained and nourished him, remembering the Church that brought him forth, remembering the blessed family which he lived in and learned from.

My beloved brothers and sisters, despite the bitter pain within us, and the inner sadness we feel deep inside ourselves, we lift our hearts to heaven and see that heaven is very great. We see that heaven is able to heal our griefs, and see the hand of God reaching out to console us all.

Blessed are you, O blessed bishop, and blessed is your monkhood, your episcopacy, your priesthood and your service. Blessed is the example you set before us.

I thank all those dear people who have comforted us and shared this pain with us. I thank the beloved fathers of the monastery, and I wish them true peace in their hearts. You are monks of the Monastery of the mighty Saint Macarius the Great. You belong to no other: you are sons and grandsons of this great saint. The Desert of Scetis, the Scetis of Macarius. You belong to no other.

Entering this monastery, great spiritual personalities arose among you and the generations passed: all of this belongs to the mighty father of monasticism, Saint Macarius the Great. Keep your peace, and keep your monasticism. Cast out anything that deviates from this.

May Christ keep you all in His mercies. May this blessed bishop remember us all in his prayers and intercessions so that we can end the days of our earthly exile in peace.

His Holiness Tawadros II,
Pope of Alexandria
and Patriarch of the See of St Mark

Monastery of Saint Macarius the Great,
Abib 24th 1734 / July 31st 2018
On the Occasion of the Funeral
of Bishop Anba Epiphanius

PREFACE

A radiant face, a benevolent smile, a source of comforting words that put to ease those who came to speak with him: this is the impression that we have as soon as the name of Anba Epiphanius is evoked.

Born in Tanta on June 27, 1954, the young Tadros Zaki Tadros graduated from the Faculty of Medicine in 1978. He entered the Monastery of St Macarius on February 17, 1984 and he was tonsured as a monk on Bright Saturday (April 21, 1984), receiving the name of Epiphanius. Soon after, his many talents quickly qualified him to lead essential positions in the monastery.

His great dedication, his helpfulness, and his affability allowed him to be the best candidate to serve and provide medical care to the sick of the monastery, within and abroad. Thus, he was chosen in 1997 to accompany Fr. Matthew the Poor to the U.S. for a heart surgery, as well as accompany Fr. John to Germany in 2002 and Fathers Luke and Panaghias to Germany in 2008 for cancer treatment. Upon his return to Egypt, he continued to care for the latter two with the utmost dedication until they were transported to the next life.

His exceptional intellectual abilities were noticed by his spiritual father, Fr. Matthew the Poor, as soon as he entered the monastery. While he was still a novice Fr.

Matthew urged him to study the Church Fathers and the Church Traditions and provided him with the necessary books for this goal. The young monk's love for tradition drove him to invest long hours reading Patristic works, ancient monastic literature, and liturgical studies. This prepared him to become entrusted with the care of the monastery library, which can now attribute most of its digital cataloguing as a result of his efforts.

His accuracy and his great capacity for work made him also suitable to contribute to the financial accounting of the monastery. He gave himself generously to this rather unappreciated task for many years, from the early 90's until his departure. His accuracy paved the way for him to revise the monastery's publications. Therefore, he was also asked to offer his help at the printing house. This gave him the opportunity to contribute many articles in *St Mark* magazine.

In 2002, as the hieromonks responsible to preside over the liturgical services became elderly, Fr. Matthew the Poor chose some monks, including Father Epiphanius, to be ordained priests to assist. Although with tears he pleaded to be exempt because of his unworthiness, the monk Epiphanius had to submit to this ordination by obedience. From then on, because of his simplicity and his spirituality, the choice fell on him and on Fr. Panaghias to concelebrate with our hegumen Fr. Cyril at all the great feasts and most Sundays of the year. At the end of every celebration, Fr. Panaghias escaped to the farm to milk the cows, to get rid of any feeling of vain glory. Likewise, Fr. Epiphanius offered his services to the humblest and to anyone who needed it.

As the librarian, Fr. Epiphanius had numerous opportunities to meet many personalities visiting the monastery. All attested to his extremely affable nature, his availability and his openness which showed in his welcoming smile that could not be imitated. Fr. Philippe Luisier said of him, "I met him when he was a librarian, and then I saw him again as an abbot and a bishop, always like himself, with that smile that was only his." Those who had the opportunity to speak with him could also measure the extent of his knowledge, which, however, did not prevent him from always considering himself a beginner. One time he was invited to deliver one of the inaugural lectures at a congress and he took his place on the stage with other important personalities. However, the next day, we saw him sitting among the audience towards the back. When invited to resume his place on the platform, he made this answer, "Yesterday I was a speaker; today I came to learn."

In 2013, following an opinion poll done at the initiative of the Patriarch, he was chosen by the majority of the monks to be the superior of the monastery and was later ordained Bishop and Abbot by the hands of His Holiness Pope Tawadros II. But he always remained himself. He never accepted that one would make a *metania* (greeting prostration) to him, rather, to those that insisted, he would say, "If you prostrate before me, I too will prostrate before you!" In the liturgy, he forbade the chanters from singing any hymns in his honor as bishop;

and he never sat on the episcopal seat (which was already only a simple chair), but he sat on the floor like his fellow monks. Throughout all the liturgies prayed within the monastery, he refused to be ornamented with typical liturgical attire associated with his rank as bishop, but he contented himself with a simple white tunic like the other priests. When questioned, he would respond that "these ornaments are made for diocesan bishops, but in a monastery we must keep our monastic sobriety." At the celebrations in which he was to anoint the congregation with oil (such as the Last Friday of Lent and Holy Saturday), Bishop Epiphanius did not wait for each one to come to him, but it was him who took the vial of oil, passed among the faithful and anointed everyone in his place. He truly embodied before us the One who told his disciples: "I am among you as one who serves" (Lk. 22:27)[1]. He considered that his main task as bishop was to preside over Sunday liturgy and to distribute to his community the Lord's Body and Blood. For him, this was how he could best contribute to achieve the ultimate goal of creation, which is "to gather together all things in Christ" (Eph. 1:10). Therefore he was never absent from the Sunday liturgy unless compelled by travel or sickness, and he would encourage his monks to follow the same example. In this, he was a worthy descendant of the bishops of the first centuries such as Ignatius, Cyprian, Irenaeus and Peter of Alexandria and, like them, he ended his life by martyrdom.

---

[1] Unless otherwise noted, all Scripture quotations are from NKJV.

FIRST FIELD OF INTEREST:
THE TRADITION OF THE DESERT

But now let us see what fields of interest were most dear to him. First, his love of the tradition of the Desert Fathers. From his early years at the monastery, he began to digitally transcribe the five Arabic volumes of St Isaac of Nineveh. After this, he worked on *Bustān al-Ruhbān* (The Garden of the Monks)[2] by verifying them on the manuscripts that we have at the monastery, by numbering the various apophthegms, and especially—and this is what took him the most time—by correlating each saying to the other collections of apophthegms preserved in the various ancient languages[3]. It is difficult to estimate how much time he had to devote to read these various collections, some of which cover several volumes. And it was not only about reading, but one had to be very careful to identify parts that have their correspondence in the Arabic *Bustān*. This work allowed him to live in the company of the Desert Fathers for long days, months and years. And by frequenting these Desert Fathers, he was, so to speak, "infected" by them and ended up

---

[2] The Coptic Arabic collection of apophthegms of the Desert Fathers.

[3] This work culminated in the first scientific edition of this Arabic collection of apothegms: al-Rāhib Ibīfānyūs al-Maqārī (ed.), *Bustān al-Ruhbān* (Wādī al-Naṭrūn: Monastery of St Macarius, 2013). This edition differs from all the others that preceded it by a continuous numbering of the different apophthegms, and by a concordance table at the end of the volume which establishes for each saying the correspondences with the other collections in Greek, Latin, Syriac, Coptic, Armenian and Ethiopian.

resembling them in their love of solitude and silence, in the great inner peace that radiated from him, in his personal asceticism and the despoliation of his cell, in his humility and his refusal of any mark of honour, in his abnegation, taking upon himself the faults of others and refraining from responding to offenses but by a surplus of love and kindness[4].

He had found in the spirituality of the Desert Fathers the Pearl of Great Price that leads straight to the Kingdom and to union with Christ. In order to transmit this same Pearl to his monks, he personally insisted to read daily the *Bustān al-Ruhbān* in the refectory. And while he read it to us, we had before our eyes a living incarnation of what we were hearing that redoubled our profit. He considered that this common and daily reading of the *Bustān* was, together with the Sunday liturgy, the best way to unify the community in the same spirit.

Second Field of Interest: the Ancient Liturgies

Another field of interest to which he was no less attached was the study of ancient liturgies. As a young monk, he was interested in finding the original Greek text of the three Anaphoras still in use in the Coptic Church (St Basil, St Gregory and St Cyril). He was fascinated by the flavour that these texts have in their

---

[4] At the monastery there existed a group of monks who opposed him. These monks had established a WhatsApp group in which they kept criticising him, often exceeding the limits of politeness. When the monks who were close to him begged him to order the closure of this group, he used to simply reply: "I respect the freedom of opinion. It is by love and not by constraint that we will gain them."

original language, making us relive in the time of the Fathers. He then published the Greek text, accompanied by an Arabic translation and many notes[5]. For the last of these liturgies (that of St Mark/Cyril), he was not content with offering the Greek text and its translation, but he studied all its primitive forms that have survived in ancient manuscripts (such as Strasbourg, Dayr al-Balāyza, Vienna, Barcelona and many others). The reader is thus invited to travel with him through time, to visit the ancient Christian communities, to attend their liturgies and to taste the fervour and simplicity of their faith. Another major liturgical source that caught his attention was the *Great Euchologion of the White Monastery,* formerly published in Coptic and French by Dom Emmanuel Lanne. He discovered a number of ancient Anaphoras that were part of our liturgical heritage yet were lost (such as those of St Matthew; St Thomas; Pope Timothy, Patriarch of Alexandria; and many others). Between 2010 and 2013, he published in a dozen articles the content of this *Euchologion* in Sahidic Coptic and Arabic, in the *Maǧallat Madrasat al-Iskandariyya,* and in 2014, he collected all the texts in one volume[6].

---

[5] al-Rāhib Ibīfānyūs al-Maqārī (ed.), *al-Quddās al-Bāsīlī* (Wādī al-Naṭrūn: Monastery of St Macarius, 2011); *Id.* (ed.), *al-Quddās al-Ġrīġūrī* (Wādī al-Naṭrūn: Monastery of St Macarius, 2013); *Id.* (ed.), *Quddās al-Qiddīs Murqus (al-Quddās al-Kīrillusī)* (Wādī al-Naṭrūn: Monastery of St Macarius, 2015).

[6] Anba Epiphanius (ed.), *Ḫūlāǧī al-Dayr al-Abyaḍ* (Cairo: Madrasat al-Iskandariyya, 2014).

Third Field of Interest: Patrology

Alongside the ancient monastic literature and the primitive liturgies, a third field of interest was Patrology. As noted earlier, as soon as he entered the monastery, he was encouraged by Fr. Matthew the Poor to deepen his knowledge of the Church Tradition and the Church Fathers. Obedient to his spiritual father, as a young monk he engaged himself in an assiduous study of classical works on Patrology and History of Dogma, by authors such as Quasten, Kelly, Torrance, Prestige, Mersch and many others. Through this, he was able to appreciate the theological and spiritual richness of our forefathers and the gap that separates us from them. One of the main causes of this distance is the difference in language and therefore the difference in cultural thought patterns. More than once, he heard his spiritual father explain how we lost our language twice. The first, losing Greek language, after the Council of Chalcedon (451). The second, the loss of the Coptic language because of the arrival of the Arabs (640). We became like children who do not know the language of their parents anymore. This realization explains why he exerted effort to perfect his knowledge of Greek, and as a bishop, he encouraged his monks to study Greek and other ancient languages. In his book "Mafāhīm Inğīliyya" (Biblical Concepts), which has been here translated for the English readers, he explains the meaning of some Greek words used in the New Testament, then he uses many texts of the Fathers to present the content with all its extent. After realising that the Masoretic text of the Old Testament that is currently used was not the text that the Fathers read, he undertook the translation in two columns, in Greek and Arabic, of the text of the Septuagint in order to remedy this. Though it was a large-scale project, he published the books of Genesis, Exodus and, now in press, Isaiah. But he also encouraged other monks of his monastery and elsewhere to edit other parts, and had himself started the revision.

FOURTH FIELD OF INTEREST: ECUMENISM

Finally, one last field of interest for him was the relations with the Christians of the other Churches. His open-mindedness, his great culture, his respect for the opinion of others, and his natural benevolence, disposed him to that. And this is why Pope Tawadros II chose him nearly twenty times to represent the Coptic Church in various conferences or symposiums. He has always honoured his Church by presenting a faithful and endearing figure.

As a good disciple of Fr. Matthew the Poor, he was convinced that unity needs to be lived before being discussed:

> Human logic would like us first to remove the differences so unity could be accomplished, whereas the logic of God, as it is expressed in the inspiration of the second chapter of the epistle to the Ephesians ('For He Himself is our peace, who has made both one, and has broken down the middle wall of separation,' Eph. 2:14), requires that unity should be accomplished first, so that the middle partition may be

broken down.⁷

That is why at all the meetings in which he participated, Bishop Epiphanius was more attentive to live the unity, to live the communion of love with his partners, rather than to discuss with them. On one occasion while he was eating at the Monastery of Bose in Italy, sitting with other bishops and church representatives, he offered this consideration: "Here we are sitting together at the same table, sharing in love the same meal. We have prayed together and we are convinced that the food we prayed upon has been sanctified by our prayer. What prevents us then from sharing together the Lord's Meal?" Another time, again in Bose, following a conference, the discussion was about the division of the churches and how to remedy these differences. While the discussion heated up, Bishop Epiphanius remained silent. Finally, the moderator said, "Let us see what the Desert Fathers have to tell us about this problem." He gave the floor to Anba Epiphanius who replied: "Forgive me, I am not a theologian and I do not understand divisions. I only understand what unity is." This response was applauded for several minutes. To some of the Bose's brothers, he made this confession: "When a baptized Christian presents himself to me to receive the

---

⁷ Matthew the Poor, 'Christian Unity', in *Id., The Communion of Love* (Crestwood, NY: St Vladimir's Seminary Press 1984): 231. Elsewhere, Fr. Matthew the Poor returns on the same idea: "It is also necessary that we live together in the one essence of doctrine before agreeing on its contents". (*Id., True Unity will Inspire the World* (Wādī al-Naṭrūn: Monastery of St Macarius 1988): 4).

Body of Christ, and believes in truth that it is the Body of Christ, I have no right to refuse him." In spite of this, his sense of communion made him respect the decisions of all the bishops of his Church, and this caused him an inner heartbreak whenever he had to decide whether or not to communicate a Christian whose Church was not officially in communion with the Coptic Orthodox Church.

THE SENSE OF COMMUNION

Having examined the interests close to his heart, it is not difficult to discover the heart, the living centre that influenced all of them. Anba Epiphanius had what is called the *sensus Ecclesiae*, that implies the sense of communion. As the Body of Christ, the Church is essentially a communion—communion through time and space. In this regard, he often explained to different listeners (for example in Bayāḍ, Egypt, in January 2018, and in Melbourne, Australia, July 17, 2018) how this doctrine of the Church as the Body of Christ had been central to St Paul and how it is inextricably linked to the sentence that was the cause of the Apostle's conversion: "Saul, Saul, why do you persecute me?" (Acts 9:4). For Anba Epiphanius, our living in Christ and Christ living in us represents the basis of all the teachings of St Paul. By listening to Anba Epiphanius one could understand not only how central this doctrine was to St Paul, but even more so how it was for himself, and how it explained his attachment to all his fields of interest.

Communion through time explains his great love for the monastic tradition. He used to live in communion with the various generations of monks who came before us from the fourth century until today. When he used to read to us the Desert Fathers' Apophthegms at the refectory, we felt that the limits of our community expanded to contain tens of thousands of holy monks who lived before us, and who, always alive, look at us from above, encourage us and live in communion with us: "For He is not the God of the dead but of the living, for all live to Him" (Lk. 20:38).

Additionally, communion through time also explains his interest in ancient liturgies in their original language. He could thus feel himself in communion with the liturgical assemblies of previous centuries. The Eucharist is the source of communion, not only with our contemporaries, but even through the centuries. "For we, though many, are one bread and one body; for we all partake of that one bread" (1 Cor. 10:17). One can even say that there is only one Eucharistic celebration, begun by the Lord on the evening of Holy Thursday that is perpetuated "until He comes" (1 Cor. 11:26).

The Church as communion through time also explains his interest in the Fathers of the Church, the richness of their theology and the resulting spiritual consequences, such as the concept of the Deification of the Christian or the concept of the Redemption by the physical union. It is by uniting with our nature, by taking us in Him, that Christ has accomplished our redemption, and it is by uniting ourselves to Him, by receiving Him in us, that we receive the effects of this redemption. This concept, common to the Fathers, was central to Anba Epiphanius, and this explains his attachment to a holy medieval Coptic bishop, Būlus al-Būšī, in whom he discovered expressions that bear witness to this same concept of redemption through physical union. More than once in Bishop Epiphanius' homilies of great feasts such as Easter or Christmas, Anba Epiphanius presented sentences of Būlus al-Būšī and those of St Cyril or St Athanasius that paralleled and corresponded with each other. He was amazed to find in the Middle Ages a holy bishop who knew how to preserve the theological and spiritual richness of the patristic golden age in spite of all the hazards that his Church underwent during this difficult time—change of language and culture, oppression, cultural and material impoverishment. Anba Epiphanius' attachment to this medieval author was no doubt due to the fact that he embodied communion through time, despite all the contrary factors, and this was precisely what Anba Epiphanius had the desire to be for his own time and what he encouraged others to become[8]. This explains the unconditional support and benevolent aid he gave to young Coptic institutions interested in theological and patristic studies, such as the *Alexandria School Foundation*, the *Holy Transfiguration College*, or the *Panarion Bookstore*. He

---

[8] Anba Epiphanius published many texts of the bishop of Būš: Anbā Būlus al-Būšī, *Tafsīr Sifr al-Ru'yā* (Commentary on the Apocalypse), Anba Epiphanius (ed.) (Wādī al-Naṭrūn: Monastery of St Macarius, 2017); *Id.*, *Mayāmir al-Aʿyād al-Ilāhiyya* (Homilies for the Divine Feasts), Anba Epiphanius (ed.) (Wādī al-Naṭrūn: Monastery of St Macarius, 2018).

helped many young people to obtain scholarships, and has encouraged many others to continue their studies in Theology or Patrology. For him, these young students represented the hope of the renewal of the Church, a Church which, in the future, will have her bonds of communion with the spiritual and theological richness of its past reinforced.

His sense of communion also explains his openness, benevolence and love for Christians of other Churches. Through the Fathers he had studied in depth the concept of the Church as the Body of Christ. He relied upon the works of Mersch[9] for the Fathers in general, and of Fr. Du Manoir for St Cyril of Alexandria[10]. This increased the acuity of his sense of communion. He understood that the Church, the Body of Christ, cannot be divided and that, despite the walls and barriers created by men, there is deep communion, as a flowing groundwater, between the various parts of the Body of Christ. It is this conviction, this perception, which guided him in all his relations with other Christians.

We can now measure the immensity of the loss we have suffered, not only at the level of our monastery or the Coptic Church, but at the level of the universal Church, the Body of Christ in the whole world. But it seems that Anba Epiphanius belonged to this category

---

[9] The work of Émile Mersch, *Le corps mystique,* was accessible to him in its English translation: *The Whole Christ* (London: Dennis Dobson, 1962).

[10] Hubert du Manoir de Juaye, *Dogme et spiritualité chez saint Cyrille d'Alexandrie* (Paris: Vrin, 1944).

of people of whom Scripture says that "the world was not worthy of them" (Heb. 11:38).

This is the will of God: in heaven he will have more influence than if he had remained with us for he can better serve the Church he loved so much. Let us have faith that the Lord knows better than us what is right, let us learn to stretch our hands out in front of Him, as we learned from St Macarius—of whom Anba Epiphanius was a worthy spiritual son—and to say with him:

"Lord, as you will, and as you know, have mercy."[11]

Monk Wadid el Macari
Monastery of St Macarius

---

[11] *Sayings of the Desert Fathers*, Macarius 19 (*Ward*: 131).

INTRODUCTION

> His countenance had a great and wonderful grace. This gift also he had from the Saviour. For if he were present in a great company of monks, and anyone who did not know him previously wished to see him, immediately coming forward he passed by the rest, and hurried to Antony, as though attracted by his appearance. Yet neither in height nor breadth was he conspicuous above others, but in the serenity of his manner and the purity of his soul.[12]

Love generates. Love is like a mother who is capable of giving birth. It is like a mother who keeps us in her warm womb, welcoming us, embracing us, nourishing us and then begets us to a new life, to the freedom of the Spirit. Love is able not only to regenerate, but also to recreate a person, wholly and completely. When we live in love we are renewed, and our whole being is renewed and transfigured because we live in God who is love and light. The Bible tells us that "God is love, and he who abides in love abides in God, and God in him" (1 Jn. 4:16), and that "everyone who loves is born of God and

---

[12] Athanasius of Alexandria, *Life of Antony*, 67 (*NPNF* 2/4: 214).

knows God" (1 Jn. 4: 7). We also know that "God is light and in Him is no darkness at all" (1 Jn 1,5). Through His love, the Holy Spirit embraced the whole creation when He generated it the first time. And Christ, the Logos of God made flesh, with His love has tenderly embraced creation when He recreated it through His Incarnation, Death and Resurrection. If we live in love, we live in the Kingdom from now.

This is the spiritual experience I had with an extraordinary man, our Father Bishop Anba Epiphanius, abbot of the Monastery of St Macarius, who had a sensibility, a delicacy, a spirituality, a charisma, a culture, a tenderness and a fatherhood which were remarkable. He was a man of meekness and light. Of this man one will never cease to say enough.

On Sunday, July 29, 2018, at about 3 a.m., as he was leaving his cell to go to the church of Saint Macarius to preside over the Divine Liturgy on Sunday, the holy abbot was struck with extreme, cold and premeditated brutality. The three blows to the neck were fatal. He was found lifeless, lying in a pool of blood, at about 4:30 a.m. His sudden and violent death shocked all those who knew him. "Why so much wickedness against this 'green wood'?", many of us asked ourselves. Why such a heinous act to so good and gentle a man, a man of such profound spirituality and such rare humility, whose gentle smile and whose words rich in wisdom have given peace and consolation to so many people all over the world? This question has torn the hearts of many of his spiritual children. Still, was it not done worse to the Lord Himself? Was He not the first to have told the women of Jerusalem, "If they do these things in the green wood, what will be done in the dry?" (Lk. 23:31). The story of Anba Epiphanius embodies the terrible and unfathomable mystery of the Cross. Did Christ fail on the Cross? Have the martyrs died in vain? As Christians we should know that the death of the innocent is seed of life. Tertullian wrote in the 2nd/3rd century *semen est sanguis Christianorum*, "the blood [of the martyrs] is the seed of Christians," which can also be translated "the blood of Christians is seed [of novelty]"[13]. This new seed of life must not be understood in a vague metaphorical sense or as a wish, but rather, in a concrete way: new life, new beginning. It is as if God, in front of this great love "to the end" (cf. Jn. 13:1), could not deny the martyr anything he asks.

Nevertheless, at the same time, the story of this bishop, meek and humble of heart, shows in itself the unmistakable traits of the Transfiguration and the Resurrection. As with Christ, for us too there is no transfiguration without each carrying his own cross and drinking his own cup: "You will indeed drink the cup that I drink, and with the baptism I am baptised with you will be baptised" (Mk. 10:39). For Christ, the Transfiguration was immediately followed by the announcement of the Passion and by the Cross itself. This means that their profound interconnection on the mystical level reveals that the Cross cannot exist without Transfiguration. The suffering and the pains of trials are only momentary

---

[13] This is how Onorato Tescari translated this phrase in a 1951 Italian edition of Tertullian's *Apologeticum* (*Società Editrice Internazionale*).

and are not the definitive reality; instead the truth is that the body is transfigured forever by the power of the Resurrection of the Lord. Our father Anba Epiphanius is the living example of these words.

It is said in the desert monasticism that depending on which trait is more evident in the life of a monk—the transfiguring light or suffering —he is called either *pneumatophoros* (bearer of the Spirit) or *staurophoros* (bearer of the cross). It may seem paradoxical that the disciples of Saint Macarius the Great—by definition 'the *pneumatophoros*'—are called in Coptic prayer books "his children, bearers of the cross". It is rare that the two faces of the mystery of Christ, suffering and glory, appear at the same time in the same person with the same intensity.

And yet Anba Epiphanius was the extraordinary case of a man of God in whom many of us, especially those closest to him, have experienced firsthand the coexistence of this mysterious combination of Cross-Transfiguration. He was a man who was radiant in his face and, at the same time, a man of sorrows. The comforting smile he was able to give to us was often overcome by tears and discouragement. Indeed, he is considered *pneumatophoros* (cf. *below*); nevertheless, he is also a true *staurophoros*. In himself he had achieved the mystery of Christ here on this earth.

With his life and his death, Anba Epiphanius gives us further confirmation of the evangelical certainty that, like the body of Christ on Mount Tabor, so too our lowly bodies, afflicted by suffering and humiliation, will be transfigured and conformed to His glorious Body, in virtue of the power that Christ has to submit to Himself all things. It is this divine promise that must give us the strength and the consolation to face the daily crucifixions on our calvaries.

Thus, a monk of our monastery, taken by the Spirit, expressed himself a few hours after the execrable crime, saying, "Open the spiritual eyes of your heart, brothers! Do you not see that all this is glory?"

REAL-LIFE STORIES
WITH THE MARTYR, BISHOP EPIPHANIUS

We at the monastery believed that we were to keep our memories and interactions with the bishop as precious jewels that were only to be told and displayed to close friends and in very unique situations.

Yet God wanted men and women from all over the world to enjoy the beauty of these pearls of true evangelical wisdom and to know this man of God, the humble man of the "last place". For, in fact, "a city that is set on a hill cannot be hidden. Nor do they light a lamp and put it under a basket, but on a lampstand, and it gives light to all who are in the house" (Mt. 5:14-15).

The extraordinary fact is that it seems as if the Lord wanted to publicly affirm His will through the Gospel pericope which was read on the occasion of the Divine Liturgy to which the body of our father the abbot was present, approximately an hour before the funeral, on August 1, 2018.

In it we read: "For there is nothing covered that will not be revealed, nor hidden that will not be known" (Lk. 12:2). Indeed, God has commanded that the time has come for everyone to know. For this reason, I allow myself to share some personal memories with the reader.

I met Abuna (father) Epiphanius when he was still a simple hieromonk and the librarian of the Saint Macarius community. It was 2009 and I was at the beginning of my monastic quest. I remember that he immediately caught my attention for his extreme simplicity, his great humility, his genuine smile, his kindness, his dedication, his rare ability to listen, and his sincere love for all Churches.

I immediately had the impression that I was in front of a man of rare spiritual and monastic stature, an authentic son of Saint Macarius the Great and of Fr. Matthew the Poor. I also realized that, as happened to a disciple of Abba Antony, 'it was enough for me to see him.'[14] Soon, I realised that this man was an extraordinary mixture of seemingly contrasting things: profound humility and great culture, seriousness in spiritual life and great joviality, asceticism and solitude mixed with a rare openness to all.

Anba Epiphanius held together numerous monastic qualities and a vast culture, scientific and otherwise, religious and otherwise. He was always careful to hide what he knew and did not talk about it until he was forced to. And even when he said something he was sure of, he always assumed that his information could be incomplete. One of the most common words in his vocabulary to which his spiritual sons had become

---

[14] Cf. *Apophthegm* 29, in *Bustān*: 23-24. *Sayings of the Desert Fathers*, Antony, 27 (*Ward*: 7).

accustomed to was "maybe". And "maybe" is one of those terms that only true scholars use.

In 2011 I visited the Monastery of Saint Macarius because I needed to photograph some of the manuscripts I needed for my research. Anba Epiphanius greeted me with his usual smile. I was amazed by the fact that he stayed with me in the manuscript room for three hours at a time while he was opening to me the folios I had to photograph one after another, without showing any discomfort. On the contrary, all the time, he told me numerous episodes concerning the monastery with his well-known sense of humour. I will never forget that blessed morning. How much we laughed together! The impression I had that day was that, for Anba Epiphanius, knowledge and study were a real vocation, at the service of which he had made available all his abilities and all his strength.

On March 4, 2013, when he was elected as abbot and bishop of the Monastery of Saint Macarius, I sent him an email to congratulate him. He answered almost immediately. He used to always reply to emails even after having taken on the heavy task of abbot and bishop, even if only with one line. He wrote me words that in retrospect I consider a prophecy of his mission as a bishop:

Beloved brother ...

The peace and love of our Lord Jesus Christ be with you. I thank you for your kind message, begging your charity not to forget me in your prayers so that the Lord may give me the wisdom necessary to serve the house of our holy Fathers and to make the hearts of all the saints rejoice in this place when they see us respecting their teachings and follow in the footsteps of their life-giving words. Send my greetings and my love to father ... asking for his prayers for me and for all my brothers in the Monastery of Saint Macarius.

Your brother,

Epiphanius el Makari

In September 2015, our beloved father Epiphanius visited the Monastery of Bose in Italy as he was invited to speak at the International Conference on Orthodox Spirituality, in which he presented a paper entitled "Forgiveness in the life of Father Matthew the Poor". On that occasion, I received from God the immense blessing of accompanying him throughout the visit and of hearing many anecdotes. Below are some stories about him.

- Many brothers and sisters of Bose wanted to talk to him and were looking for the right opportunity to do so. All those who had this possibility came out of the meeting with him full of joy, carrying in their hearts words of life to preserve. More than one person told me that the words that they had been told by Anba Epiphanius were just what they needed at that time. We were all amazed at the great wisdom that had been given to this man. Just as happened to Abba Antony, of whom Saint Athanasius tells us: "Who came [to him] troubled with doubts and did not get quietness of mind?"[15]. Some monks began to bring back to the prior of Bose their personal anecdotes with Anba Epiphanius and the words he had told them. The anecdotes became more and more numerous and enjoyable, and the prior began to notice

---

[15] Athanasius of Alexandria, *Life of Antony*, 87 (*NPNF*, 2/4: 219).

the joy painted on the faces of those who had met him, both of the monks and of the guests. For this reason, it was decided to collect all his 'apophthegms' in a booklet for internal use. For the monks of Bose these apophthegms represented the natural extension of the sayings of the ancient Desert Fathers. We thank the Monastery of Bose for having authorized us to publish them. The reader will find them in the appendix to the book. It will be immediately noticed that they have the same spirit as the sayings of the ancient Fathers of whom Anba Epiphanius was a faithful son.

- The monks were so struck by the extreme simplicity and humility of this man that they dedicated a commemorative tile with his name on it that was inserted in the so-called "wall of the *pneumatophores*," which contains the names of the spiritual people who visited the monastery leaving a particular impression on the community. The following year, in 2016, during the International Conference on Father Matthew the Poor, organized on the occasion of the tenth anniversary of his departure, Anba Epiphanius was able to see the tile. Struck by all this love for him, he said to the monks: "Why did you do it? I do not deserve it! I am your brother and I really love you. But I do not like these honours. I just want you not to forget me in your prayers".

- There was a phrase that he often repeated to the monks of Bose during the 2015 conference, that he drew from a story on Saint Macarius contained in *Bustān al-Ruhbān*, the Coptic-Arabic collection of the apophthegms of the Desert Fathers: "I have not yet become a monk but I saw monks"[16]. There was certainly something to wonder about: how could a bishop, superior of one of the oldest monasteries of Christianity, say such a sentence? The phrase aroused even more astonishment in view of the fact that many saw him as a clear model of what it means to be a monk. In this sense, a person in Bose even went so far as to confide to me that "Anba Epiphanius is the only person I have seen in my life who deserves to be called a monk".

- Also during his 2015 visit, which was full of anecdotes and stories, a debate followed after his speech. Anba Epiphanius sat on the platform together with other speakers and the moderator who gathered the questions from the audience. With a thorny question on the causes and possible solutions for the division that currently exists between the Churches, a long exchange of opinions and replies began, most of which were pessimistic with respect to a solution to the problem that had enormous dogmatic, historical and political implications. Throughout the discussion, Anba Epiphanius remained silent, without comment. Finally the moderator said: "Let us hear what the Desert Fathers have to say about this issue. What does Your Grace think of the division of the Church?" Anba Epiphanius replied with burning words: "Forgive me, I am not a theologian. I do not understand divisions. I only know what unity is". A great liberating applause sealed the wisdom of the desert.

---

[16] Cf. *Apophthegm* 37, in *Bustān*: 28-29. Cf. *Sayings of the Desert Fathers*, Macarius, 2 (*Ward*: 125-126).

- During his session the public sent many questions in the form of leaflets, many of which were not asked due to lack of time. During the break, one of the organisers noticed that one of the leaflets concerned him personally, took it and handed it to Anba Epiphanius. It was written:

> Earlier today we heard Bishop Epiphanios from the Monastery of Matthew the Poor speaking. It was like a breath of fresh air blowing across a barren field. His words on forgiveness and mercy radiated love. Should we not adopt this simple approach to obtain greater understanding between the Churches and not continue to carry the baggage of the past?
>
> Joan Cassaignon

At the end of the session, coming out of the conference room, he was approached by the world famous patrologist Norman Russell, a great expert on St Cyril of Alexandria, together with his wife. After having warmly greeted him and thanked him for his words, Russell's wife, Mrs. Joan Cassaignon, said to him: "Father, thank you so much for your wonderful words. In truth, I had sent a leaflet to the organizers to read it but unfortunately there was no time." With his proverbial simplicity, Anba Epiphanius took the leaflet out of his pocket and said with a smile, "Was it this by chance?" Mrs. Cassaignon's face lit up with a big smile and a burst of joy. It was then that she told Anba Epiphanius: "You are the only one who gave me hope in the unity of the Churches and the only one who did not make me yawn during the speech!"

– The "beacon of monasticism,"[17] our father Anba Epiphanius, was very faithful to a monastic principle which he never renounced, which is not distinguishing himself in anything from his brothers. The anecdote we are about to tell will better clarify what we mean. One of the monks at Bose organized a monastic *collatio* with Anba Epiphanius. The meeting took place after dinner, while sipping a cup of tea, in a warm and friendly atmosphere. The monk handed out glass cups for tea and gave Anba Epiphanius a different cup, one that was larger and made of ceramic. Several times Anba Epiphanius asked one of the novices to move the tea cup that had been set before him, citing various excuses: "I need the space here in front of me. Please, could you take it off?" The novice insisted that he keep it in front of him, so that he could sip his tea. Finally, the cup was removed. After a presentation made by the monk, Anba Epiphanius inaugurated the *collatio* like this:

> As soon as I entered I noticed that you had put a huge ceramic tea cup while all of you have a normal glass. So a story came to my mind that is found in the apophthegms of the Desert Fathers that I will now tell you:
>
> "It is said of Saint Pachomius that he was once working with his brothers and that this work required that each of them carry a large quantity of bread. One of the young men said to him: 'Never let it be that you bring something, Father. Behold, I bring what is enough for me and for you together.' The saint replied: 'Never let this be. If it has been

---

[17] "Beacon of monasticism" is a title that the Coptic euchological texts attribute mainly to Abba Antony and Abba Macarius.

written of the Lord that He want-ed to resemble His brothers in everything (cf. Heb 2:17), how could I, the ignoble, distinguish myself from my brothers so as not to carry my burden like them.'"[18]

Do you understand the spirit in which we start? No discrimination. We all–young and old–are beginners in the way of Christ.

– At the end of 2015 I asked him: "My beloved Father, absolve me. Give me a word to live with today." And the answer was: "You do not need a word because you are united to the living Word. May He fill you, keep you and encompass you." I had the impression then that his words would make me live not only for one day but for many days to come.

A True Spiritual Father

If spiritual fatherhood means something, to me it means this: the ability of a person with a long and painful spiritual and human experience, to recreate, to continuously regenerate, through love, another person with a view to the Kingdom of Heaven. The love I felt before this bishop and spiritual father who fought to the last breath to stay an authentic monk, faithful to his vocation, was of such purity, simplicity, and harmony that it made me say that this will be the air we will breathe in the Kingdom of Heaven. It cannot but be so.

If Christ resembles someone, I think He has many traits of Anba Epiphanius: his peace, his smile, his radiant eyes with tears when he was moved, his paternal and

---

[18] *Apophthegm* 75, in Bustān: 48.

loving voice, his sense of humor, his spiritual intelligence. His strength was in his profound humanity. He was a monk in the true sense of the word because he did not lose his humanity. On the contrary, his humanity was transfigured through his monastic vow, his prayer, his asceticism, his faithful communion in the Holy Mysteries, his love and his service to all. His fully deified humanity made him looked at all things and at all people through the light of God that permeates the whole creation. And this is how he saw all things pure.

The secret of Anba Epiphanius consisted in the "eschatology of everyday life". Every thought, every action, every desire was directed towards the coming of the Lord and towards the moment of the terrible and blessed encounter with the luminous face of the risen Christ. As the life of St Macarius says:

> He was thinking to himself, as was his custom, about his passing away and his meeting God and the judgment that would be passed against him at that time[19].

More than once we heard him say, "When I see Him face to face [i.e. Jesus Christ], what shall I tell Him?" On June 10, 2016, on the occasion of the Divine Liturgy commemorating Fr. Matthew the Poor's departure, a day after the Feast of the Ascension, from the lectern of the church of Saint Macarius, Anba Epiphanius quoted a passage from his spiritual father:

> The true monk is he who continually lives the feast of the

---

[19] *Bohairic Life of Saint Macarius*, 34. Cf. Tim Vivian (ed.), *Saint Macarius the Spiritbearer* (Crestwood, NY: St Vladimir's Seminary Press, 2004): 192.

Ascension, who, all his days, is content with what is above, with the Spirit and the Truth. He fears nothing on earth: neither distress, nor persecution, nor famine, nor nakedness, nor peril, nor sword (cf. Rom. 8:35). He desires nothing on earth (cf. Ps. 73:25): neither honour, nor particular friendships, nor supremacy, nor power, nor praise, nor names, nor appearance, nor titles. In fact, he mysteriously feeds on what is above: on the food of Truth and on the drink of love. All those who feed on these two things forget what belongs to this world, they forget their families, their countries, and even themselves. Every person in Christ desires the life of the world to come, according to the words of the Creed. The monk, however, brothers, already lives it because he died to this passing world. Ascension is not only the feast of us monks, it is our daily work towards this world. It is the only life that remains to us.[20]

This was Anba Epiphanius' "manual of life" and he was killed for his Christian consistency. He was killed because the "face to face" with the Almighty was his only polar star. Not worldly glory, not honours, not recognition, not compromises with evil.

The blood of this man of God cries; it cries for forgiveness, for purification, and for a new beginning. If he has taught us one thing, it is that love, even if it seems defeated, "never falls" (ἡ ἀγάπη οὐδέποτε πίπτει, 1 Cor. 13:8), i.e. it remains standing, it is never in vain, it is never useless, it is never a loss of time, expression of weakness or fragility. It always bears fruit, always, even when it is not understood, when it is beaten, insulted or

---

[20] Matthew the Poor, "Ṣuʿūd al-Masīḥ", in *Id.*, *al-Qiyāma Wa-l-Ṣuʿūd* (Wādī al-Naṭrūn: Monastery of St Macarius 2000): 380.

killed or crucified or, even, and above all, when it is addressed to the enemies. Indeed, this man was for many the living example of him who loved his enemies to the end. You can cover the light, you can try to turn it off, you can try to suffocate it, to disguise it, but if it is connected to the divine Power Plant, your every attempt is futile. It is like trying to put out a fire with a beach bucket.

This was the spiritual father and life-teacher Epiphanius, in an age in which spiritual fathers are scarce. Every opportunity was good to learn something from him. We have even learned from his silences and from the expressions his face took on. As Palladius wrote in the first pages of *Lausiac History*, this ancient collection of stories from the Egyptian desert:

> Teaching does not consist in the harmony of words and syllables—sometimes men possess these who are as vile as can be—but in meritorious acts of character, cheerfulness, intrepidity, bravery, good temper; add to these, unfailing boldness, which generates words like a flame of fire. For if this had not been so, the great Teacher would not have said to His disciples: "Learn from me, for I am meek and lowly in heart" (Mt. 11:29).[21]

It is amazing how we can meet people with whom we are in such harmony that it almost seems like something we do not deserve. People whose company we feel we do not deserve. They are people so beautiful and so pure that they reveal our selves to ourselves. Their love,

---

[21] Palladius, *Lausiac History*, trans. by W. K. Lowther Clarke (New York: Macmillan Company, 1918): 38-39.

which surrounds us and illuminates us, also reveals all our dark sides that we do not want to see. Yet they do not ever judge us, but rather accept us and warm us. Simply, they "infect" us with their beauty. This is the strength of the saints. These qualities derive from Christ Himself. As the Scripture says: "Of them the world was not worthy" (Heb. 11:38). Indeed, we were not worthy of this meek man, of this *kalógeros*, this "beautiful elder," a title which is applied in the monastic writings to those elders who have particularly radiated the pure beauty of the Spirit.

THE BOOK THAT IS IN YOUR HANDS

A tenacious reformer of monasticism and a tireless creator of bridges of unity among the Christian Churches, Anba Epiphanius was also an internationally respected scholar of biblical, liturgical and patristic texts. He has published numerous books that have enriched the Christian library in Arabic. About this you have read more extensively in the preface to this volume written by the monk Wadid.

In English we have so far by Anba Epiphanius his synthesis of the spiritual and human heritage of Father Matthew the Poor, re-founder of the Monastery of St Macarius the Great[22] and some other papers he delivered on the occasion of the international symposia he

---

[22] The paper was entitled "The Human and Spiritual Legacy of Father Matthew the Poor 1919-2006" and was delivered at the Saint Athanasius College (SAC) in Melbourne, Australia, a couple of weeks before he died. The article will be published in the proceedings of the conference, to appear at the end of 2020.

participated in.[23]

This book that has been translated here into English (Arabic title: *Mafāhīm inğīliyya* "Biblical Concepts") is the fruit of the work of many people we would like to thank here: first of all the translator Samuel Kaldas, but also David Georgy and all those who helped us deliver this book to the English-speaking world in a proper way. We hope that this book will be the first in a long series and will help to raise awareness of the personality and spirituality of Anba Epiphanius. This book is an anthology of his exegetical meditations of some "biblical notions" which the author himself has prepared, and which was published in Arabic by the Monastery of St Macarius' press in May 2018, a few months before his passage to Heaven. The different chapters appeared earlier as articles when he was still a young monk in the magazine of the monastery *Saint Mark*, starting from the 1990s, and were partly revised in view of the publication of this anthology. Some of these articles have been excluded so as not to further weigh down the volume, but they will certainly be published on future occasions. The author also gave a precise outline to the articles, preferring a soteriological concatenation to a chronological arrangement. In fact, they have been arranged with regards to the first coming of God in history, when, in the fullness of time, Christ became incarnate of the Virgin Mary, until the moment when the last trumpet sounds and there will be the second and final coming of God in History, when, in the fullness of fullness—if we can

---

[23] Cf. "Some Significant Dates".

say— the Judgment will take place and those who have been justified will live forever with the Holy Trinity in the heavenly Jerusalem. In this sense the approach is very similar to an important anthology of Anba Epiphanius' spiritual father, Fr. Matthew the Poor, the first book that has been translated into English: "The Communion of Love" (St Vladimir's Seminary Press 1984). This book therefore follows step by step the announcement of the end of history, with the first coming of Jesus Christ and the eruption of eternity into its painful folds, until the moment of the sudden interruption of the course of history and the revelation of blessed eternity, with the second and glorious coming of Christ. At the centre of this book is the Death and Resurrection of the Lord Jesus Christ, the pinnacle and summit of God's infinite love for humanity, and the pouring out of the Holy Spirit into the hearts of those who believe in Christ. Starting from the meditation on the gifts and charisms of Pentecost, Anba Epiphanius moves to outline the effects of salvation on us. In particular, the chapter on the conversion of St Paul shows the centrality that spiritual experience must have in our lives and in our preaching. The life "in Christ," of which St Paul speaks to us, is nothing but the restitution in words, as far as this is possible, of his personal and shocking experience of the risen and glorious Christ. It does not take long to realize that this principle has inspired the whole life of Anba Epiphanius himself. The profound emotion with which the abbot once spoke of the conversion of St Paul makes us say with certainty that he experienced a similar event of grace that has forever transformed his existence. This grace led him to experience the mystical union with Christ, so important to him that he often said that "without this mystical union, our Christian life has no value."

The anthology, therefore, expresses some *leitmotivs* of Anba Epiphanius. First of all, the absolute centrality of Scripture in his life. For him it is the indispensable daily nourishment that keeps us constantly united to Christ and through which we grow in His knowledge. In his perspective, the linguistic and historical-literary background has a fundamental importance for a serious exegesis that takes into account the complexity of the text and the context in which the simplicity of God is revealed.

In doing this, he uses all possible tools. First of all, the in-depth study of ancient biblical languages (especially Hebrew and Greek) is always the privileged tool for the critical understanding of the scriptural text. Anba Epiphanius accustomed his monks not to blindly trust any translation because every translation, however good, is always limited and experimental. His homilies, although rare, never lacked the use of original texts. As he often said of himself, he was not a homilist. He was and remained a serious exegete and this was clearly evident from his homilies from the ambon. In the book, therefore, more often than not, we will realize that the argument is based on a single word, and analyzed, studied in its original language, followed as an Ariadne's thread. It is essential to arrive at a precise understanding of the letter of the text in order to understand its spiritual meaning.

And here we come to another fixed point: Anba Epiphanius had great respect and love for the Old Testament. Against the background of his New Testament speeches there is almost always the Old Testament without which the "so great a salvation" (Heb. 2:3) wrought by Christ would not be understood. However, he always uses it as a premise, a necessary premise but still a premise, to the announcement of the fulfilment of salvation achieved by the Lord and to the transmission of this salvation to us. God's assumption of our human nature, His life-giving Death and His glorious Resurrection are the exegetical key of all Scripture because Christ, the Theanthropos, is the Alpha and Omega, the centre of everything. And we dare to say, we are at the heart of the heart of everything: we are the recipients of all that the Lord, in His great goodness, has worked and continues to work. It is thanks to His coming in the flesh that today we can become partakers of the divine nature (cf. 2 Pt. 1:4).

Furthermore, there is a very important aspect that needs to be emphasized. Despite his approach of great scientific seriousness, which meant that he did not fear, for example, contemporary critical exegetical studies, Anba Epiphanius always tried to insert his exegetical research into the traditional understanding of the text, resorting both to patristic exegesis, in particular to the Alexandrian Fathers, and to the liturgical practice of the Church, particularly the Coptic. For Anba Epiphanius, in order for the Bible to be understood, it must be studied and read critically. However, it is not a simple philological reality. It remains above all the living Word of

God that must be prayed and ruminated upon in the depths of the heart.

In this sense, the spiritual factor is certainly the centre of his research, since primacy remains of the Spirit who is the only One to guide the reader towards "the thought of Christ", to reveal the mystery of Christ hidden in the lines. For this reason, for our father the bishop it is necessary to remain adherent to an ecclesial understanding of Scripture, since it is not a dead letter, but life in action, "for the word of God is living and powerful, and sharper than any two-edged sword" (Heb. 4:12), lived in the ambit of the Church.

It is certainly another manifestation of his profound search for communion, which was discussed in the preface to this volume. His exegesis represents an extraordinary encounter between ancient and modern, between consolidated traditional data and new critical perspectives in the philological, historical, literary, philosophical and archaeological fields. Among other things, it should be noted that many of these articles were, in their rudimentary form, only simple notes for personal meditation and the study of Scripture.

Starting from the search for the multiple meanings even of a single term, the Spirit disclosed Scripture to Anba Epiphanius as one opens a precious treasure box of which the key has been found. It is this biblical and exegetical treasure that Anba Epiphanius was able to deliver to us before he was accepted into the heavenly glory.

The Beauty that "Infects"

When our beloved Father Epiphanius was still alive, I continually prayed to the Lord that he could "infect" more and more people with his beauty. After his sudden death, which tormented us with grief, I discovered that the number of those who loved him was enormous. It was then that I realized that God had answered my prayer. In fact, Anba Epiphanius was the "grain of wheat" that died to the world and that brought much fruit.

Despite his only five years as a "public figure," he managed to create a family around him, as well as a school made up of all those who loved him and who wish to continue his mission. If it is true that "precious in the sight of the Lord is the death of His saints" (Ps. 116:15), how much more will the death of his martyrs —of the perfect witnesses of His love—be!

If the Lord does not know how to say no to the plea of a martyr, we are certain that He will not deny to Anba Epiphanius what he has always sought in life and in death: a true, sincere, committed monasticism that seeks only Christ; a united Church, from East to West, around Christ, Her only head; a new generation of men and women seriously engaged in study, deepening, and research, in order to rediscover the beauty of the hidden treasures of the rich monastic, patristic and liturgical tradition of the Egyptian Church.

As he used to say to young people:

Don't just talk and blame others for the wrong. The wrong will be put right. You are a generation full of good.

Read, study, translate, learn. I have high hopes of you[24].

While we are well aware that such a man is unique and cannot be replaced, we plead the Holy Trinity not to leave the Monastery of Saint Macarius and the universal Church orphans of him, and to arouse for us other luminous persons like him, giving those who knew him to witness the beauty of this man, a clear mirror of the beauty of Christ, and a scent of good perfume of the Risen Christ.

And to the Holy Trinity glory, honour and power, to the Father, to the Son and to the Holy Spirit, for ever and ever, amen.

Monk Markos el Makari
Monastery of St Macarius the Great

Baramhat 1st 1735 / March 10th 2019
Sixth Anniversary of Anba Epiphanius'
Episcopal Consecration

---

[24] *St Mark Foundation for Coptic History Studies*, n.d.: 19.

SOME SIGNIFICANT DATES

June 27, 1954: Anba Epiphanius was born in Tanta, Egypt.

1973: He began to take spiritual retreats at the Monastery of Saint Macarius.

1978: He graduated in medicine at the University of Tanta.

February 17, 1984: He entered the Monastery of Saint Macarius the Great.

April 21, 1984: He was ordained a monk on the eve of Bright Saturday (Holy Saturday).

October 17, 2002: He was ordained a priest by the hand of Anba Mikhail, Metropolitan of Assiut and superior of the monastery at that time.

September 17-22, 2012: He participated in his first International Conference on Coptic studies, sponsored by the Sapienza University of Rome, with a paper entitled "The Adam Doxologies of the Matins according to the Manuscripts of the Library of the Monastery of Saint Macarius".

March 10, 2013: He was ordained bishop and abbot of the monastery by the hand of His Holiness Pope Tawadros II, based on the election of the majority of the community and the recommendation of Anba Mikhail.

April 18, 2013: He was installed in the monastery on the eve of the Feast of the Cross in the presence of forty bishops of the Holy Synod.

September 7-9, 2014: He participated as a delegate of H.H. Tawadros II in the international symposium "Religions and Cultures in Dialogue," sponsored by the Community of Sant'Egidio and held in Antwerp (Belgium), with a paper entitled: "The Believer is a Man of Friendship".

September 6-8, 2015: In Tirana (Albania) he participated, again as delegate of H.H. Tawadros II, in the international symposium "Religions and Cultures in Dialogue," sponsored by the Community of Sant'Egidio, with a paper entitled: "Martyrs, the New Face of Christianity".

September 9-12, 2015: He participated as a guest speaker at the 23rd International Conference on Orthodox Spirituality, organized by the Monastery of Bose in Italy, with a paper entitled: "Forgiveness in the Life of Father Matthew the Poor".

May 21-22, 2016: He participated in the first international conference on the figure of Fr. Matthew the Poor entitled, "Father Matthew the Poor: a Contemporary Desert Father," organized by the Monastery of Saint Macarius and the Monastery of Bose, with a paper entitled: "The Spiritual and Human Heritage of Father Matthew the Poor, Ten Years after his Repose".

September 3-16, 2016: He participated as a delegate of H.H. Tawadros II, in the Congress of Benedictine abbots held in the Abbey of Saint Anselm on the Aventine (Rome). He presented a paper entitled "Monasticism and Christian Unity".

September 18-20, 2016: He was again the representative of H.H. Tawadros II at the annual international symposium organized by the Community of Sant'Egidio "Religions and Cultures in Dialogue," which was held in Assisi. He presented a paper entitled "Mercy in Practice: Feeding the Hungry, Giving Water to the Thirsty".

November 28 - December 1, 2016: He participated in Vienna in a session of the Commission for the ecumenical meeting between the Eastern Orthodox Churches and the Catholic Church (CEE) at Pro Oriente with a paper entitled: "Obstacles on the Way to Full Unity".

September 6-9, 2017: He participated as a guest speaker at the 25th International Conference on Orthodox Spirituality, organized by Monastery of Bose in Italy, with a paper entitled: "Receiving the Enemy in the Desert Fathers".

September 10-12, 2017: In Münster (Germany) he participated for the fourth and last time at the annual international symposium organized by the Community of Sant'Egidio "Religions and Cultures in Dialogue," with a paper entitled: "Martyrdom, Memory and Reality of Christians".

February 27 – March 1, 2018: He participated in Vienna in a session of the Commission for the ecumenical meeting between the Eastern Orthodox Churches and the Catholic Church (CEE) at Pro Oriente with a paper entitled: "Report on Coptic Church about Changes, Challenges and Ecumenical Highlights".

July 13-16, 2018: He participates as a guest of honour in an international conference organized by Saint Athanasius College (SAC) in Melbourne, Australia, with a paper entitled: "The Human and Spiritual Legacy of Father Matthew the Poor 1919- 2006".

July 29, 2018: He was killed at dawn between his cell and the church of Saint Macarius.

THE FULLNESS OF TIME

> But when the fullness of the time had come, God sent forth His Son, born of a woman, born under the law, to redeem those who were under the law, that we might receive the adoption as sons (Gal. 4:4, 5).

'For everything there is a season, and a time for every matter under heaven' (Eccl. 3:1); so declares Solomon the wise in the book of Ecclesiastes. He perceives that there is 'a time to be born, and a time to die', and that God 'has made everything beautiful in its time' (Eccl. 3:2, 11). The angel Gabriel spoke to Daniel the prophet concerning God's plan and His providence in determining the times and seasons, telling him of the time God had appointed for the coming of the Lord Jesus:

> Seventy weeks of years are decreed concerning your people and your holy city, to finish the transgression, to put an end to sin, and to atone for iniquity, to bring in everlasting righteousness, to seal both vision and prophet, and to anoint a most holy place (Dan. 9:21–24).

In a similar manner, after His baptism in the Jordan, we find the Lord Jesus beginning His ministry declaring: 'The time is fulfilled' (Mark 1:15). St Paul also affirms the fullness of time when he says: 'But when the fullness of the time had come, God sent forth His Son, born of a woman' (Gal. 4:4).

But what does this expression *the time is fulfilled* mean? And what did St Paul intend by his phrase *the fullness of time*? Does it refer to a random date? Or does it rather indicate that the world had now become ready, more than ever before, for God to intervene and for the awaited coming of Christ?

It would be difficult for us to fully grasp what St Paul meant by *the fullness of time*. But if we attempt to study the condition of the world at the time of Jesus' birth and the circumstances that facilitated the rapid spread of the Gospel, we will be better able to understand some of the meanings that Paul had in mind.

The Spiritual Condition

The Jewish people had been dreaming for many centuries of a king from the lineage of David who would restore Israel's former glory. But as they suffered one military invasion after another from their neighbouring peoples, their hope for the coming of this earthly king had all but disappeared. Consequently, a different hope was born among them for the coming of a king with divine attributes, as Isaiah the prophet had declared to them:

> For unto us a Child is born, unto us a Son is given; and the government will be upon His shoulder. And His name will be called Wonderful, Counsellor, Mighty God, Everlasting Father, Prince of Peace. Of the increase of His government and peace there will be no end, upon the throne

THE FULLNESS OF TIME

of David and over His kingdom, to order it and establish it with judgment and justice from that time forward, even forever (Isa. 9:6, 7).

This King would come in 'the Day of the Lord,' judge Israel's enemies, and establish peace and justice among His people Israel:

> Therefore the Lord says, the Lord of hosts, the Mighty One of Israel, 'Ah, I will rid Myself of My adversaries, and take vengeance on My enemies. I will turn My hand against you, and thoroughly purge away your dross, and take away all your alloy. I will restore your judges as at the first, and your counsellors as at the beginning. Afterward you shall be called the city of righteousness, the faithful city' (Isa. 1:24–26).

Nor was it Isaiah the prophet alone who awoke this hope in them. The prophet Ezekiel also delivered a message from God, declaring to the people that God Himself would come down to shepherd His people Israel:

> And the word of the Lord came to me, saying, 'Son of man, prophesy against the shepherds of Israel, prophesy and say to them, "Thus says the Lord God to the shepherds: 'Woe to the shepherds of Israel who feed themselves! Should not the shepherds feed the flocks? You eat the fat and clothe yourselves with the wool; you slaughter the fatlings, but you do not feed the flock. The weak you have not strengthened, nor have you healed those who were sick, nor bound up the broken, nor brought back what was driven away, nor sought what was lost; but with force and cruelty you have ruled them. So they were scattered because there was no shepherd; and they became

food for all the beasts of the field when they were scattered. My sheep wandered through all the mountains, and on every high hill; yes, My flock was scattered over the whole face of the earth, and no one was seeking or searching for them.'

'Therefore, you shepherds, hear the word of the Lord: "As I live", says the Lord God… I will require My flock at their hand; I will cause them to cease feeding the sheep… Indeed I Myself will search for My sheep and seek them out. As a shepherd seeks out his flock on the day he is among his scattered sheep, so will I seek out My sheep and deliver them… I will feed My flock, and I will make them lie down," says the Lord God' (Ezek. 34:1–15).

Until the birth of Christ this hope had grown dim, at least among the priestly orders whose religion consisted in nothing more than carrying out ritualistic duties and preserving the decaying traditions of their elders. This hope lived on only in those devout souls who were awaiting the coming of the Christ, and who lived in this hope every day. A good representative of this group of souls who waited expectantly for the Lord's promises is Simeon the Elder, who 'was just and devout, waiting for the Consolation of Israel.' After he had taken the child Jesus into his arms, he blessed God and said: 'My eyes have seen Your salvation which You have prepared before the face of all peoples; a light to bring revelation to the Gentiles, and the glory of Your people Israel' (Luke 2:25–32). When the pious woman Anna, the daughter of Phanuel, who lived upon this hope, learned of the Lord's coming, she also 'gave thanks to the Lord, and spoke of Him to all those who looked for redemption in Jerusalem' (Luke 2:36–7). Yet the priests whose task it was to study the Law and discern the times and seasons, because they were preoccupied with their own private concerns, failed to recognise the fullness of time in which God had determined to visit His people.

There were some, however, who held a different understanding of the Messiah's coming; namely, that God would come in the time He had determined not only to visit His people and save them from the hands of their enemies, but also to pour out His wrath on the wicked and take vengeance on the transgressors. Thus, John the Baptist who came to prepare the way of the Lord, whose coming and appearance in the wilderness paved the way for the fullness of time, warned the people that the Messiah's coming would be for retribution on those who worked evil:

> Brood of vipers! Who warned you to flee from the wrath to come? Therefore bear fruits worthy of repentance… I indeed baptise you with water unto repentance, but He who is coming after me is mightier than I… He will baptise you with the Holy Spirit and with fire. His winnowing fan is in His hand, and He will thoroughly clean out His threshing floor, and gather His wheat into the barn; but He will burn up the chaff with unquenchable fire (Matt. 3:7–12).

Indeed, John the Baptist came to prepare the way for the Messiah, but the condition of the people had sunk to such a state, especially among the priests and leaders of the congregation, that he was forced to announce to them the imminent coming of the Lord for retribution. The Law (Torah) which constituted the cornerstone of the life of the Jewish people had become a tool wielded by the priests and Pharisees to judge matters according to their own private interests and personal whims. The Law which had come down to assist the people in their salvation had now become a hard and merciless master. And so, instead of a source of guidance and direction in the spiritual way, the Law itself became the way in which we thought we could gain favour in God's eyes.

The Pharisees had turned the Law into a heavy burden which they laid upon the people's shoulders by appointing themselves as overseers and compelling the people to fulfil the Law and respect the customs through their own interpretations and explanations which they imposed. In this way, the Law deprived the people of the joy of life, and created an awareness of sin and transgression and the impossibility of fulfilling the Law's difficult requirements. It was for this that Jesus rebuked the Pharisees when He said, 'They bind heavy burdens, hard to bear, and lay them on men's shoulders; but they themselves will not move them with one of their fingers' (Matt. 23:4). So too the Apostle Paul wrote to the Galatians, reminding them that the Law 'was added because of transgressions… For if there had been a law given which could have given life, truly righteousness would have been by the law,' and that 430 years before the coming of the Law, Abraham lived in peace with God through faith. The Law, as used by the Pharisees, accomplished nothing for the people but to bring them under a curse and condemnation (cf. Gal. 3:6–21).

The cries and groans of the people under the burden of the Law and its hard yoke and the lack of spiritual direction from their leaders were important factors that paved the way for the fullness of time and the speedy coming of the Saviour, just as the people's cry on account of their oppression in Egypt brought about the fullness of time for the economy of their salvation, their exodus from the land of Egypt, and the sending of Moses the prophet for their redemption (cf. Ex. 3:7–10).

THE POLITICAL AND CULTURAL CONDITIONS

It is likely that the Apostle Paul also intended *the fullness of time* to refer to the political and cultural situation of the world at that time. For the world was indeed culturally prepared for the manifestation of the Messiah. Greek had become the language of culture throughout the whole civilised world, that is, throughout the Roman Empire. This language assisted the apostles and evangelists to swiftly spread the message of the Gospel, far better than the Hebrew or Aramaic languages which were only spoken in Palestine.

As for the political situation, the *pax Romana* prevailed throughout the whole world; lines of connection were ready, accessible and even safe. This allowed the apostles to travel both by land and sea within the bounds of the Empire, even to Rome itself to preach Christ there. For although apostles faced persecution, the Roman state was prepared to tolerate any new religion.

The Greek philosophers themselves, through their teachings, had paved the way for the acceptance of this new religion which would bring them peace and furnish them with the life of that 'ideal city' they were calling for.[25]

Within the borders of the Jewish state, the political state of affairs was in the grip of labour pains, and in dire need of the Messiah's appearance. Christ was born in the days of Herod the Great, a king who represented the very essence of evil for he used his authority to crush any rebellion, whether real or imagined. He shed the blood of forty-five members of the Jewish Council (the Sanhedrin) at the beginning of his reign, just as he had slain his wife, his mother-in-law, and three of his brothers out of envy. Even when he was at death's door, he commanded a number of notables from among the people to be executed in order to ensure that there would be a great mourning in the city on the day of his departure.[26]

And let us not forget the measures he took after the return of the Magi who had gone to worship the Child of the manger, how he commanded the murder of all the male children of Bethlehem to ensure the destruction of the Child King of whom the Magi and even the priests had told him would be born in Bethlehem. Herod thus truly represents 'the prince of this world', who stirred up all his powers to murder the innocent Child

---

[25] Cf. J. W. Shepard, *The Christ of the Gospels: An Exegetical Study* (Grand Rapids, MI: Eerdmans, 1971): iii–ix.

[26] *Ibid.*, 40.

THE FULLNESS OF TIME

of the manger. In him that saying of John the Evangelist is realised, that the light came into the world and shone in the darkness, and the darkness did not comprehend it (cf. John 1:5). Indeed, it was in the reign of King Herod that *the fullness of time* drew near for God to show His power and declare His presence.

THE DISCIPLES AND APOSTLES

It can also be said that God was preparing vessels for Himself beforehand, and that He therefore made them ready to take a role in *the fullness of time*, as the Apostle Paul explains in his letter to the Galatians: 'But when it pleased God, who separated me from my mother's womb and called me through His grace, to reveal His Son in me, that I might preach Him among the Gentiles …' (Gal. 1:15–16). If Christ was to be preached, there was need of people like Peter and Andrew, James and John, Aquila and Priscilla, that the word of salvation might be spread abroad and the coming of the Messiah announced to the people. There was an especial need for a person like the Apostle Paul, the likes of whom are rarely seen in any age, who brought together the faith of the Jews, the learning of the Greeks and the citizenship of a Roman, so that he could preach the Gospel without hindrance and travel through all the regions of the world announcing the good news of salvation. Indeed, God found in Saul of Tarsus, who became Paul the Apostle, a chosen vessel to bear His name before Gentiles, kings and the children of Israel (cf. Acts 9:15).

ANBA EPIPHANIUS

Finally, God was preparing for Himself in the fullness of time a holy virgin girl, worthy for Him to take flesh in her womb, and to be entrusted with the mystery of the Incarnation. This virgin was seen by the prophet Isaiah seven hundred years before the Incarnation, for he prophesied saying: 'Behold, the virgin shall conceive and bear a Son, and shall call His name Immanuel' (Isa. 7:14). Ezekiel the prophet also saw her in a vision, saying, 'This gate shall be shut'—a prophecy of her virginity—'it shall not be opened, and no man shall enter by it, because the Lord God of Israel has entered by it; therefore it shall be shut' (Ezek. 44:2).

This might have been what St Paul intended when he wrote to the Galatians of *the fullness of time*, and the Lord Jesus before him, when He declared that *the time is fulfilled*. But we believe that when God perceived that the time had come—that this was the appointed moment and the acceptable time—God sent His Son to the world to redeem those who were in the world, that we might attain adoption as sons.

A BRANCH FROM
THE ROOT OF JESSE

'There shall come forth a Rod from the stem of Jesse, and a Branch shall grow out of his roots' (Isa. 11:1). Anyone who considers this prophecy of Isaiah's cannot help but notice that it seems to clash—however superficially—with the verses that come immediately before it at the end of the tenth chapter:

> Behold, the Lord, the Lord of hosts, will lop off the bough with terror; those of high stature will be hewn down, and the haughty will be humbled. He will cut down the thickets of the forest with iron, and Lebanon will fall by the Mighty One (Isa. 10:33–34).

In these verses Isaiah is referring to the forests of Lebanon, renowned for their towering and ancient cedars which here symbolise the Assyrian nation with all the greatness and splendour it then possessed. When he speaks of these trees being cut down, he is indicating the decline of the Assyrian Empire. Cedar trees are evergreen, but when they are cut down close to the earth, they do not put forth branches, but wither and die. Isaiah's tree (cf. 11:1), on the other hand, which was torn down to its roots, shall sprout anew, and put forth a new branch from its roots.

Isaiah's prophecy about a tree which will sprout anew has a special prophetic significance; it is not simply an allegorical comparison of the kingdoms of Assyria and Israel. The prophecy refers to the house of David; the phrase 'stem of Jesse' is a reminder that the house of David traces its roots back to Bethlehem, where David lived as the son of Jesse, and where he was born and raised. The prophecy reveals that the star of David's house will fade, and that kingship will pass away from it. But Isaiah prophesies that the kingdom will be restored to this line once more—it shall have a new beginning, as new growth from the root of the tree.

A Historical Overview

The immediate background of Isaiah's message about a new beginning for David's kingdom is the confrontation between Isaiah and King Ahaz. Ahaz, the king of Judah, was in a desperate predicament. The kings of Syria and Israel had formed an alliance against the armies of Assyria. When Ahaz rejected the king of Israel's call to join his alliance, Israel and Syria joined forces to attack Jerusalem, intending to kill Ahaz and appoint another king over Judah who would be willing to ally himself with them. And so, when their two armies laid siege to Jerusalem, and Ahaz realised the terrible fate that threatened the city and its people, 'his heart and the heart of his people were moved as the trees of the woods are moved with the wind' (Isa. 7:2).

At this point, Isaiah the prophet met with Ahaz and delivered a message to him from the Lord. The message had two parts: the first was an exhortation to Ahaz not to fear the two kings allied against him—Rezin, king of the Arameans (the king of Syria) and Pekah, king of Israel. Isaiah tells him, 'thus says the Lord God: [the plot that they have made against you] shall not stand! Nor shall it come to pass!' (Isa. 7:7). So that Ahaz might be persuaded in his heart of this message, the prophet instructed him to ask for a sign or wonder from God, but the king refused.

The second part of the Lord's message had to do with the king's lack of faith in God's message to him, that God was able to save him from the kings allied against him: 'If you will not believe, surely you shall not be established' (Isa. 7:9). Ahaz's response had consequences beyond his personal reign: as a result of his refusal to trust God's words the kingdom of David itself would fail. Despite God's warning, the king refused to believe in His promises. For this reason, God saw fit to give Ahaz a sign of His own choosing, a sign particularly suited to His own character, which would point to His own eternal design: 'Therefore the Lord Himself will give you a sign: Behold, the virgin shall conceive and bear a Son, and shall call His name Immanuel' (Isa. 7:14).

Isaiah then describes in a prophecy the birth of Ahaz's own child; a child through whom God gives further assurance to Ahaz that he should not fear Israel and Syria: 'For before the child shall have knowledge to cry 'My father' and 'My mother', the riches of Damascus and the spoil of Samaria will be taken away before the king of Assyria' (Isa. 8:4).

In the ninth chapter, Isaiah revisits and recounts again the warning which was given to the king: namely, that if he refused to believe the words of God, the kingdom of David would come to an unavoidable end. The prophet then prophesies the birth of a son to David's house, who would establish the kingdom of David forever:

> For unto us a Child is born, unto us a Son is given; and the government will be upon His shoulder. And His name will be called Wonderful, Counselor, Mighty God, Everlasting Father, Prince of Peace. Of the increase of His government and peace there will be no end, upon the throne of David and over His kingdom, to order it and establish it with judgment and justice from that time forward, even forever. The zeal of the Lord of hosts will perform this (Isa. 9:6–7).

There seems to be a contradiction here: Isaiah had told King Ahaz that the kingdom of David would not be established, but in these verses he declares the birth of a son to David's house who was to establish David's kingdom. This contradiction is particularly apparent in the first verse of the eleventh chapter: 'There shall come forth a Rod from the stem of Jesse, and a Branch shall grow out of his roots' (Isa. 11:1). The stem of Jesse is a symbol of the house of David which will be cut down to its roots, while the Branch is a sign of the renewed continuance of the kingdom.

A BRANCH FROM THE ROOT OF JESSE

A Natural Phenomenon

The question now is whether Isaiah was expecting a miracle from God to occur, through which the kingdom and throne of David would be saved from extinction, or was he instead expecting that the kingdom would endure as a natural phenomenon, as happens when a branch grows up from the roots of a tree?

It is clear that Isaiah was referring to the natural process through which some trees are able to grow anew. Such trees, despite being cut down, are restored to life by the growth of new branches from their roots which remain in the earth. This phenomenon was not unknown to Job, who said:

> For there is hope for a tree, if it is cut down, that it will sprout again, and that its tender shoots will not cease. Though its root may grow old in the earth, and its stump may die in the ground, yet at the scent of water it will bud and bring forth branches like a plant (Job 14:7–9).

Isaiah was probably familiar with the properties of the olive trees which grew in large numbers in the region of Palestine, and which the Bible mentions more than fifty times. Although olive trees grow very slowly, they can live for more than a thousand years. Olive trees are remarkable in that, even when cut down to the ground, new branches grow from the roots around the stem and bear fruit again. This peculiarity belongs not only to the olive tree, but is found in many others—for instance, fig, walnut and pomegranate trees—as well as grapevines, which are cut down whenever they no longer bear good fruit. When the roots of these plants are watered, they put forth new branches in the following year and bear new fruit.

Certainly, Isaiah drew a lesson from nature when he presented his prophecy about the growth of the Branch that would allow the kingdom of David's house to endure. He was not speaking about the yearly pruning of trees which was carried out to encourage more vigorous growth in the trees. He was referring to the ability of some trees to return to life even after being cut down to the ground.

Nevertheless, Isaiah's message was understood as a message from God, for it confirmed the faithfulness of God which He had promised to David, that his kingdom would endure forever: 'And your house and your kingdom shall be established forever before you. Your throne shall be established forever' (1 Sam. 7:16). It is worth noting that Isaiah did not infer or extract this prophecy from his experience of the natural phenomena occurring around him; rather, nature provided him with an illustration of what God was about to do to establish David's kingdom forever, even after the kingship had vanished from his house. Thus, even though David's kingdom will come to an end through the descendants of Ahaz, it would rise anew through the Branch that will grow from the root of Jesse.

Fulfilment of the Prophecy

It is remarkable that Isaiah's prophecy, in all its details, was not fulfilled anywhere except in the person of the

A BRANCH FROM THE ROOT OF JESSE

Lord Jesus. For the child Jesus was born of St Mary the Virgin, who was of the line of David, in Bethlehem, the city of David the son of Jesse. In Him the verse was fulfilled: 'There shall come forth a Rod from the stem of Jesse, and a Branch (*nēṣer*) shall grow out of his roots' (Isa. 11:1). The Gospel of St Luke tells of the divine arrangement which led St Joseph and the Virgin Mary to Bethlehem, where the Child Jesus was born.

On the other hand, St Matthew's Gospel tells us that after the Lord Jesus was born in Bethlehem, the Holy Family fled to Egypt, and then returned and settled in the city of Nazareth, for which reason Jesus was called a Nazarene. Biblical scholars consider it likely that the name Nazareth derives from the Hebrew word *nēṣer*,[27] which means branch. The prophet Jeremiah also clearly calls the Lord Jesus branch, when he foretells the rise of a king from the line of David whose task it will be to establish His kingdom forever: "'Behold, the days are coming", says the Lord, "That I will raise to David a Branch of righteousness; a King shall reign and prosper, and execute judgment and righteousness in the earth. In His days Judah will be saved, ("for He will save His people from their sins," Matt. 1:12), and Israel will dwell safely; now this is His name by which He will be called: THE LORD OUR RIGHTEOUSNESS'" (Jer. 23:5–6). What man of David's line fulfilled this prophecy and was called

---

[27] Translator's Note (from now on TN): Scientific transliteration of Biblical Hebrew and Greek is based on the recommendations given by the *Society of Biblical Studies*, with minimal adaptations.

'the Lord our Righteousness' apart from the Lord Jesus 'who became for us wisdom from God—and righteousness and sanctification and redemption' (1 Cor. 1:30) and 'who was given up for our sins, and was raised for our being made righteous' (Rom. 4:25)?[28]

According to the prophet Zechariah, Christ is the Branch of the Lord: 'Thus says the Lord of hosts, "Behold, the man whose name is the Branch: for he shall grow up in his place, and he shall build the Temple of the Lord"' (Zech. 6:12). This is precisely the name Isaiah gave Him also: 'In that day the Branch of the Lord shall be beautiful and glorious, and the fruit of the land shall be the pride and glory of the survivors of Israel' (Isa. 4:2).

And lest the people of Israel become confused and try to apply Isaiah's prophecies to some king of David's line, Isaiah declares in a way that leaves no room for doubt that the one born from the stem of Jesse shall possess divine attributes; that is, He shall be at once both God and man. We do not know what state Isaiah was in when he uttered this prophecy; was he fully aware or in a sort of rapture? Perhaps he entered into a divine realm which rendered all his earthly senses and human abilities useless, and was granted a heavenly sense able to keenly discern the force of the words he was uttering. Hear him now, speaking of the Son of David who will establish the kingdom:

> For unto us a Child is born [of our own flesh and blood],

---

[28] TN: Slightly modified RSV.

A BRANCH FROM THE ROOT OF JESSE

unto us a Son is given [He is a Son to us because He shares our human nature] and the government will be upon His shoulder. And His name will be called Wonderful, Counselor, Mighty God, Everlasting Father, Prince of Peace. Of the increase of His government and peace there will be no end, upon the throne of David and over His kingdom, to order it and establish it with judgment and justice from that time forward, even forever. The zeal of the Lord of hosts will perform this (Isa. 9:6–7).

Indeed, this is the zeal of the Lord of Hosts: the Lord who loved His own, loved them to the end, and sent His only begotten Son to take flesh from the Virgin and take our human nature, bearing in His body our sins and all that belongs to it, so that He might grant us all that belongs to Him, and so that just as He became a son to men, He could grant us the ability to become children of God in Him. And as He became a branch—or rather, a true vine—we are made into firm branches in Him, nourished by His sap and bearing His fruits, for He says 'I am the vine, you are the branches. He who abides in Me, and I in him, bears much fruit...' (John 15:5).

This is the Branch that sprouted from the stem of Jesse, to bear the tree of Jesse and the entire house of David in His body. He did not establish the earthly house of David, but instead, through His body, opened the way to the Kingdom of Heaven to all of David's house and line, the New Israel, that is, to all who believe in the name of the Son of God.

CHRIST THE FIRSTBORN

The word *firstborn* occurs many times in Holy Scripture, referring sometimes to the firstborn of a human being, firstborn of an animal, or even the firstborn of plants and crops. According to the commandments which God gave to the Old Testament prophets, the firstborn child had a special place in the Old Testament, both within his family and before God. When the Apostle Paul wrote his letter to the Colossians, he reminded them that Christ is "the firstborn of all creation" (Col. 1:15). But what does he mean by this title, and in what way is Christ the firstborn of creation?

The Greek word for firstborn is *prōtótokos*, which literally means 'firstborn son'. It is a word peculiar to the Septuagint translation of the Old Testament, for though it does not occur in any Greek texts before the Septuagint, it is used there more than 130 times, meaning 'firstborn son; the son who is born first'. It is a translation of the Hebrew word *bᵉkōr*, meaning *firstborn* and referring to the firstborn child of a human being or an animal. Its plural form—*bᵉkōrîm*—is used for first fruits of plants.[29]

In the New Testament, the word only occurs eight times. It appears twice as a plural (Heb. 11:8; 12:23), but

---

[29] Cf. Wilhelm Michaelis, 'πρωτότοκος,' *TDNT*, VI:871–76.

the remaining six instances of the word are in the singular, all referring to the Lord Jesus. When we read the verses in which the word occurs, there is nothing particularly difficult about understanding its meaning; most of the time, it corresponds to the Old Testament concept of the *firstborn*, i.e. a firstborn son; the son who is born first. It occurs in the account of the Lord Jesus' birth of the Virgin Mary in the Gospel of Luke: 'And she brought forth her firstborn Son, and wrapped Him in swaddling cloths, and laid Him in a manger... as it is written in the law of the Lord, "Every male who opens the womb shall be called holy to the Lord"' (Luke 2:7, 23). It is worth noting that the Greek word for firstborn here (*prōtótokos*) refers to what precedes it, not what comes after it. It means that the child born here is the first to one be born, but not necessarily that he will be followed by other siblings later.[30] The word *firstborn* is also applied to Christ as 'the first firstborn among the dead' and 'the firstborn among many brethren' (Rev. 1:5; Rom. 8:29).

However, we begin to see how difficult it is to understand this word 'firstborn' when we come to a verse in St Paul's letter to the people of Colossae, and again in the letter to the Hebrews: 'But when He again brings the firstborn (*prōtótokos*) into the world, He says: "Let all the angels of God worship Him"' (Heb. 1:6).

---

[30] Cf. J. B. Lightfoot, *The Epistle of St. Paul to the Galatians*, (Grand Rapids MI: Zondervan, 1962): 271.

CHRIST THE FIRSTBORN

The verses which appear in Colossians (Col. 1:15–20) represent a hymn or poetic canticle, which many scholars consider to have been part of the liturgical or ritual prayers of the early church. This poem seems to revolve around the first word of the Hebrew Old Testament—($b^e r\bar{e}'\check{s}\bar{\imath}t$) 'in the beginning'—which carries both the sense of a *beginning* and of a *head* ($r\bar{o}'\check{s}$). The poem is divided into two sections, the first of which (Col. 1:15–17) presents Christ as the origin of creation:

> He is the image of the invisible God,
> The firstborn over all creation.
> For by Him all things were created that are in heaven and that are on earth,
> visible and invisible,
> Whether thrones or dominions or principalities or powers.
> All things were created through Him and for Him.
> And He is before all things, and in Him all things consist.

The second part of the hymn (Col. 1:18–20) presents Christ as the origin of the *new* creation, or the spring of redemption:

> And He is the head of the body, the church,
> Who is the beginning, the firstborn from the dead,
> That in all things He may have the preeminence.
> For it pleased the Father that in Him all the fullness should dwell,
> And by Him to reconcile all things to Himself, by Him,
> Whether things on earth or things in heaven,
> Having made peace through the blood of His Cross.

A close reading of both parts of the poem reveals that they are in fact two poems, parallel to one another with correspondent meanings. In the first part, Christ is revealed as the visible image of the invisible God, and the cause of all creation, whether material or immaterial. He is the establishment of the creation and all the creation depends upon Him. In the second half of the poem, Christ, however, is shown to be the mediator through which the creation is reconciled to its Creator. He is the origin of the Church, responsible for Its existence and entity. Both parts of the poem clearly indicate that Christ is not a part of the creation, but its Creator, who called it into existence from nothing; just as He is shown not to be a part of the Church, but her origin and founding cause. In these verses, then, Christ is both the God who creates and works in the creation, and its reconciler and redeemer (Col. 1: 15, 19).

THE CONCEPT OF THE FIRSTBORN IN THE OLD TESTAMENT

In order to understand the meaning of the word *firstborn* which Paul used, we must go back to the meaning of that word in the Old Testament.

In the Old Testament, the firstborn is always the firstborn *son*, even if he has sisters who were born before him; the firstborn is always a male. This firstborn — the first male child — holds a preeminent position in the family, and takes up his father's place as leader of the household at the father's death; he is also entitled to a double portion of inheritance.

CHRIST THE FIRSTBORN

The firstborn was considered the personal property of God: 'Consecrate to Me all the firstborn, whatever opens the womb among the children of Israel, both of man and beast; it is Mine' (Ex. 13:2).

The birthright or right of primogeniture[31] was at the discretion of the father himself, and not simply determined by the order of a child's birth. The father had the right to take away the birthright from his eldest son and grant it to another of his children instead. For example, in the Book of Genesis (cf. Gen. 25:29–34), the eldest son had the authority to sell his birthright to his younger brother, as Esau sold his birthright to Jacob; however, their father Jacob did not acknowledge this transaction, and asked Esau to go hunting and prepare him a meal that he might eat it and bless him, disregarding the agreement Jacob and Esau had made with one another (cf. Gen. 27:19).

In the next generation, Jacob did not give the birthright to his eldest son Reuben, but gave it to Joseph instead, the son of his beloved wife Rachel. He clearly demonstrated this when he made Joseph a robe of many colours to distinguish him among his brethren (cf. Gen. 37:3–4). As part of this special distinction, Jacob gave Joseph the right of the firstborn, which aroused the jealousy of his brothers against him, especially when Joseph told them of his dreams which suggested he would be ruler over them. Even Joseph, who was considered a

---

[31] TN: i.e. the right of the firstborn son to inherit his father's place.

firstborn son, when he presented his own two sons to his father Jacob to be blessed, presented the younger son rather than the eldest (Gen. 48:13–20).

Again, we sometimes find the word *firstborn* used in the Old Testament to refer to a son who will become a leader or will become illustrious in some way rather the natural firstborn son. When God asked Abraham to offer Isaac to Him as a burnt offering, He said to him, 'Take your only son Isaac, whom you love' (Gen. 22:2), even though Isaac was not Abraham's only son. What is meant here by *only son*—and by implication, firstborn—is *beloved* son. In the books of Micah and Zechariah also, what is meant by firstborn son is a son beloved of his parents, or precious in their sight:

> With what shall I come before the Lord, and bow myself before God on high? ... Shall I give my firstborn for my transgression' — that is, my beloved son — 'the fruit of my body for the sin of my soul? (Mic. 6:6, 7).

> And I will pour on the house of David and on the inhabitants of Jerusalem the Spirit of grace and supplication; then they will look on Me whom they pierced. Yes, they will mourn for Him as one mourns for his only son, and grieve for Him as one grieves for a firstborn' — that is, for his beloved son (Zech. 12:10).

Yet another sense of *firstborn* that is encountered in the Old Testament is when God calls Israel His firstborn in His discourse with the prophet Moses: 'Then you shall say to Pharaoh, "Thus says the Lord: 'Israel is My son, My firstborn'"' (Ex. 4:22). This is the same meaning used by Jeremiah the prophet: "For I am a Father to Israel, and Ephraim is My firstborn" (Jer. 31:9). The sense of firstborn in both these verses — a sense which does not recur subsequently anywhere in the Old Testament — does not imply that God gave birth to Israel, but means rather that Israel holds pride of place among all peoples in God's eyes; a favoured and chosen people, a people close to His heart. If anyone sins against this people, it is as though he has wronged God Himself, and must bear the punishment of his sin. Thus in the book of Exodus, when Pharaoh refuses to let Israel go, the Lord says, 'let My son go that he may serve Me. But if you refuse to let him go, indeed I will kill your son, your firstborn' (Ex. 4:23).

Finally, we find that the king who is to come and reign from David's throne will be called 'the firstborn son': 'He shall cry to Me, "You are my Father, My God, and the rock of my salvation." Also I will make him My firstborn, the highest of the kings of the earth' (Ps. 89:26–27). It is also clear that here, this firstborn son is not the result of a fleshly birth, but rather that God shall *make him* His firstborn, that is, He will make him higher than all the kings of the earth. The firstborn son, in this context then, refers to the place of pre-eminence, honour and glory which the Davidic king will occupy.

CHRIST: FIRSTBORN OF CREATION

Taking this into consideration, when St Paul presents the hymn which describes Christ as 'Firstborn of all creation', the sense of 'firstborn' he has in mind is 'the head and the beginning'; in other words, a place of prominence and exaltation higher than all created things, material and immaterial, and as the source and fountain of redemption. Based on the psalms just mentioned (Ps. 89:26–27), which is considered a prophecy of Christ, Christ is the first in God's household, and that God has made Him an heir and ruler over all the kings of the earth.

And just as the verse in Colossians designates Christ as the firstborn of all creation, it also identifies Him as the *creator* of this creation: 'For by Him all things were created that are in heaven and that are on earth, visible and invisible' (Col. 1:16).

The hymn goes on to call Christ 'the firstborn' a second time, but with a different meaning: 'the firstborn of the dead'. For He is the first to rise from the dead to eternal life without end. Even though there were some who rose from the dead before Christ's Resurrection, all of them rose to only a temporary life which ended with a second death. But Christ is the first fruits or the head of those who will rise from the dead unto life eternal with God.

Thus, we find that St Paul does not use the word *firstborn* in its literal sense, but rather uses it in the meaning that is most prominent in the Old Testament. For Christ is the firstborn of creation, not in the sense that He is created, but rather in the sense that He is creation's head and the first in God's household, whether of the old creation or of the new creation in Christ. He leads the whole household and is the first in everything therein. He is not a part of the material creation, nor even of the new, redeemed creation, but the Image of God, in whom dwells all the fullness of divinity (cf. Col. 2:9).

The Blessings of 'the firstborn' upon the New Creation

Christ Himself benefits nothing from being 'the Firstborn', but the benefit redounds to us. He is a Firstborn *to us*, for He became a brother to us by dispensation,[32] which is to say, He became the firstborn among many brethren (cf. Rom. 8:29). Also, He is a Firstborn for us with respect of His Resurrection from the dead, that He might prepare the way for us to enter into His heavenly glories.

St Athanasius the Apostolic writes:

> God, being first Creator… next becomes Father of men, because of His Word dwelling in them. But in the case of the Word the reverse; for God, being His Father by nature, becomes afterwards both His Creator and Maker, when the Word puts on that flesh which was created and made, and becomes man… [W]hen He put on a created nature and became like us in body, reasonably was He therefore called both our 'Brother' and 'Firstborn'. For though it was after us that He was made man for us, and our brother by similitude of body, still He is therefore called and is the 'Firstborn' of us, because, all men being

---

[32] TN: i.e. the Divine Economy or Plan of Salvation, as in Eph 1:10, '…that in the dispensation (*oikonomía*) of the fullness of the times He might gather together in one all things in Christ.'

lost, according to the transgression of Adam, His flesh before all others was saved and liberated, as being the Word's body; and henceforth we, becoming incorporate with It, are saved after Its pattern… [For He is] 'the Only-begotten' because of His generation from the Father, as has been said; and Firstborn, because of His condescension to the creation and His making the many His brethren.[33]

St Cyril the Great writes:

When He brings the firstborn into the world, He says: 'Let all the angels of God worship Him.' How then did He enter into the world? For He is separate from it, not so much in respect of place as of nature; for it is in nature that He differs from the inhabitants of the world: but He entered into it by being made man, and becoming a portion of it by the incarnation. For though He is the Only-begotten as regards His divinity, yet, as having become our brother, He has also the name of Firstborn; that, being made the first-fruits as it were of the adoption of men, He might make us also the sons of God.[34]

We also read in St Cyril's works:

On account of the Father's philanthropy for His creatures, the Son called Himself "Firstborn of all creation" (1 Cor 1:15)… He is therefore Firstborn for our sake, that the entire creation, grafted onto Him, might sprout from Him Who always is.[35]

---

[33] Athanasius of Alexandria, *Against the Arians* 2:61–62 (*NPNF* 2/4:381–2).

[34] Cyril of Alexandria, *Commentary on Luke*, Sermon I, trans. R. Payne Smith (Oxford: Oxford University Press, 1859): 9.

[35] Cyril of Alexandria, *Treasury of the Holy and Consubstantial Trinity*, Ch. 25 (PG 75:405c). Translated from the original Greek

CHRIST THE FIRSTBORN

St John Chrysostom writes:

For the branch by its adherence draws in the fatness, and the building stands because it is cemented together. Since, if it stands apart it perishes, having nothing whereon to support itself. Let us not then merely keep hold of Christ, but let us be cemented to Him, for if we stand apart, we perish. 'For they who withdraw themselves far from You, shall perish' (Ps. 72:27 LXX), so it is said. Let us cleave then unto Him, and let us cleave by our works. For he that keeps my commandments, the same abides in Me (John 14:21) in substance. And accordingly, there are many images whereby He brings us into union. Thus, if you mark it, He is the Head, we are the body: can there be any empty interval between the head and body? He is a Foundation, we a building: He a Vine, we branches; He the Bridegroom, we the bride; He the Shepherd, we the sheep; He is the Way, we they who walk therein. Again, we are a temple, He the Indweller; He the Firstborn, we the brethren; He the Heir, we the heirs together with Him; He the Life, we the living; He the Resurrection, we those who rise again: He the Light, we the enlightened. All these things indicate unity; and they allow no void interval, not even the smallest.[36]

---

text.

[36] John Chrysostom, *Homilies on 1 Corinthians* 8.7 (*NPNF* 1/12:47).

CHRIST THE LIGHT OF THE WORLD

> Then Jesus spoke to them again, saying, 'I am the light of the world. He who follows Me shall not walk in darkness, but have the light of life' (John 8:12).

Darkness Reigns

Before Christ came and revealed Himself as the light of the world, spiritual darkness reigned on the earth. As the divine light was veiled, the power of darkness oppressed much human nature to the extent that it gave birth to a groan that the saints hid away in their hearts, just as it is written of the righteous Lot: 'For that righteous man, dwelling among them, tormented his righteous soul from day to day by seeing and hearing their lawless deeds' (2 Pet. 2:8).

The darkness of sin was a mighty fortress in the city of death, the land of our wretchedness. From the tower of this fortress, the Enemy of the human race could send his arrows down upon the people, as he also was able—so long as he reigned from this dark tower—to find a point of entry through which he could inject his darkness into the human soul until it penetrated man's entire being.

Through the work of darkness in man, sin was able to give life to 'the old man', after the divine image had been blotted out (cf. Col. 3:9-10). In the domain of darkness, the powers of death had free reign to scatter and destroy the human flock, to such an extent that they became rulers and controllers of man's desires. These desires became the preferred tools by which the Enemy of Goodness could breathe the poison of his malice into the heart of man, causing man's way to become corrupt. Thus, Scriptures says, 'So God looked upon the earth, and indeed it was corrupt; for all flesh had corrupted their way on the earth' (Gen. 6:12). Even the powers of thought and intention, and the natural instincts—all of which were created good—were placed at the enemy's disposal; he put his yoke upon them, so that they became fuel for the fiery flame of lust that burns in man's inner being for 'every intent of the thoughts of his heart was only evil continually' (Gen. 6:5).

Due to the darkness of the sons of men, the face of humanity became adorned with sweat from years of toil, and misery and deprivation prevailed. Humanity became filled with weariness and suffered from weakness and emptiness of soul. Moreover, the darkness dug for itself deep trenches in the earth of the human soul, into which the Enemy cast the seeds of his tares that they might bring forth fruit. Because darkness reigned and sin possessed the body's members, lust dominated its instincts, and darkness lorded over the human being who had been cast out from God's presence. Humanity had fallen from the heights of living communion with God in Paradise to the lowest depths of the dust, as the Lord had said to Adam: 'For dust you are, and to dust you shall return' (Gen. 3:19).

Humanity's bitterness was pushed even further by the sense of destitution and spiritual bankruptcy, of deprivation from all spiritual inheritance. The whole human race became 'a people robbed and plundered; all of them are snared in holes' (Isa. 42:22).

Darkness spread thick clouds over the face of the earth, covering all who dwelt therein: 'For behold, the darkness shall cover the earth, and deep darkness the people' (Isa. 60:2).

Hope Renewed

As humanity felt its utter poverty and the death that infected its existence, humanity lifted its face hoping for salvation. Thus, Jacob, the father of the tribes says, expecting salvation: 'I have waited for your salvation, O Lord!' (Gen. 49:18).

This desperate hope for salvation and light remained alive in the persons of the prophets. David the Prophet cries: 'Restore us, O God; cause Your face *to shine*, and we shall be saved!' (Ps. 80:3). He entreats, saying: 'Oh, send out *Your light* and Your truth!' (Ps. 43:3). He continues to cry out, 'Make Your face shine upon Your servant; save me for Your mercies' sake. Do not let me be ashamed, O Lord, for I have called upon You' (Ps. 31:16–17).

ANBA EPIPHANIUS

God Responds to Humanity's Cry

God looked upon the darkness and dejection of humanity, lamented at its state of humiliation and responded to the cry of the dejected. His answer came on the lips of the prophets who spoke with the Spirit of God to announce the *imminent coming of the Light* that would make recompense for years of toil and hardship, and exchange humanity's misery and the bitterness of its slavery for the sweetness of release from the bonds of darkness. The prophets told of the coming rescue from the snares of death and the restoration to God of a humanity that had been drowning in the darkness of grief.

Job the Righteous rejoiced at the dawning of light, upon his life and his salvation from the pit of perdition, saying: "He will redeem my soul from going down to the Pit, and *my life shall see the light*" (Job 33:28 LXX).

The Prophet Isaiah comforted the soul of humanity, declaring to her: '… *your light* has come! And the glory of the Lord *is risen has dawned* upon you' (Isa. 60:1). He also announced the good news to those who were sitting in darkness, saying, "'The people who walked in darkness have seen *a great light*; those who dwelt in the land of the shadow of death, upon them *a light has shined*' (Isa. 9:2).

Likewise, Nahum the Prophet preached warmth unto hearts frozen over with the icy coldness caused by distance from God: 'On a cold day, *the sun rises*' (Nah. 3:17 [LXX]).

CHRIST THE LIGHT OF THE WORLD

Zechariah the Prophet announced to a weary humanity, upon whom darkness had settled like a perpetual evening, 'At evening time it shall happen that it will be light' (Zech. 14:7).

So also Malachi the Prophet cried out in joy at the humanity's healing from the illnesses of the darkness of sin and from the famine of righteousness by the shining rays of the Sun of Righteousness, saying, 'The Sun of Righteousness shall arise with healing in His wings' (Mal. 4:2).

THE MANIFESTATION OF THE LIGHT

At last, in the fulness of time, Christ came and declared Himself the true light that comes forth from the Father—'I came forth from the Father and have come into the world' (John 16:28)—energised and moved by the hidden power of love within Him, yearning to save humanity from the tyranny of darkness and to destroy the obstacles that had arisen due to man's disobedience.

Christ came as the radiance of God's glory to drive away the heavy fog that lay over the hearts of men. He came to liberate them from the chains of darkness that held them fast and overpowered them, 'to open their eyes, in order to turn them from darkness to light, and from the power of Satan to God' (Acts 26:18). He came to remove the restraints of darkness from human souls and to enlighten all the souls imprisoned behind the walls of the darkness of slavery to the passions, 'to bring out prisoners from the prison, those who sit in darkness from the prison house' (Isa. 42:7).

He came to grant comfort to the weary and distressed, and to those for whom, because of the abundance of their despair, life had come to seem like a night with no coming dawn. He came to bear the burden of all the hearts that were being crushed under the weight of worries and sufferings, calling them saying, 'Come to Me, all you who labour and are heavy laden, and I will give you rest' (Matt. 11:28).

The True Light came as the power of a new life in order to halt the stream of transgression spreading throughout humanity's being, and to lift up and deliver all those who were drowning in the oceans of darkness, and give new life to those who had been swept away in the current of death: 'Have mercy on me, O Lord! Consider my trouble from those who hate me, You who lift me up from the gates of death' (Ps. 9:13); 'I have come that they may have life, and that they may have it more abundantly' (John 10:10).

On the Threshold of Perceiving the Entrance of the Light

So long as there are no obstacles on the side of man that might hinder and prevent the Light from entering and working, it begins its work immediately. Though it might work slowly and gradually, its effect becomes clearer and more obvious day after day.

When the Light enters the heart, with the assistance of the Spirit of God—according to the verse, 'If you live by the Spirit you put to death the deeds of the body, you will live' (Rom. 8:13)—a man begins to put to death 'the old man' with all his old traits and passions, clearing the field for the seed of the new man to grow and develop. Then the image of the new man, created according to God in righteousness and the holiness of truth begins to appear. And as the life-bearing Light enters the heart, the current of life pours through the heart like an overflowing river that sweeps all remaining traces of darkness. For this reason, Christ is called 'The light of Life'; that is, He is the light that bears life in its rays and bring life to those in the deadness of sin to raise them from the dead, as is mentioned in the Gospel of John, 'He who follows Me shall not walk in darkness, but have the light of life' (8:12).

The Light never stops working, as the Lord says, 'My Father has been working until now, and I have been working' (John 5:17). Christ continues His work until the soul weans herself off the former pleasures and desires from which she used to drink without satisfaction. Through the unceasing activity of the Light, the soul's readiness to listen to the promptings of lust and the urgings of the passions decreases, until the day comes when a man tramples them under his feet, nauseated by all the works of darkness, for 'a soul satisfied [by the work of the Light] loathes the honeycomb' (Prov. 27:7). The soul finds her true satisfaction in the Word of God which is Light, and in the means of grace that nourish the seed of the inner life.

When a person surrenders and submits to the working of the Light, the Light banishes every inward

ANBA EPIPHANIUS

anxiety and fear, replacing them with peace, calmness, joy and ease of conscience. Christ Himself promises, 'Peace I leave with you, My peace I give to you' (John 14:27). And as is the nature of light, the Light illuminates the spiritual path before a person, leading his steps along the way of peace, 'to guide our feet into the way of peace' (Luke 1:79). Moreover, Scripture proclaims, 'Your word is a lamp to my feet and a light to my path' (Ps. 119:105). The Light also rouses our attention, warning us of every obstacle and pit of perdition, 'For the Lord will be your confidence, and will keep your foot from being caught' (Prov. 3:26).

Sons of the Light and Sons of the Day

A person who lives in darkness must either attempt to shake off the authority of Light so that he can continue in sin, or else set his heart to walk along the road towards the Light. Darkness begins to retreat before the power of the Light's work, step by step, until the Light conquers the heart and fills every corner of it. It becomes a strong support and mighty helper to all who strive and struggle against the vanities of the world's darkness.

The work of Light does not end at help and support; for He even leads the charge into the line of fire in the raging battle between the kingdom of light and the kingdom of darkness in order to repel the attacks of sin. The Light reveals His work as divine power when He puts an end to the work of unseen enemies and halts the fiery darts directed towards the children of God by the forces of darkness for 'He has shown strength with His arm; He has scattered the proud …' (Luke 1:51). It is promised that 'God is our refuge and strength' (Ps. 46:1) and 'For with authority and power He commands the unclean spirits, and they come out' (Luke 4.36).

From the coming of Christ to this day and even until His second coming, the war between Light and darkness continues without any truce. For this reason, the Lord commands us and warns us: 'Walk while you have the light, lest darkness overtake you' (John 12:35). Nonetheless, it is a cause of joy for us that through the Divine Light's presence in our world, God's kingdom has been revealed—a kingdom of everlasting Light. The Light came to this earth and will not depart from it, but rather It has spread outwards and grown deeper until It has penetrated man's very nature and granted him a new birth. The attributes of the Light developed within man until a new man took shape and was brought forth—a man with a new nature and good gifts from the Father of Lights (cf. James 1:17). When the Light poured forth upon this earth, human nature was no longer sick or barren, for now the wheat of humanity's righteousness was filled with ears of grain, which is the life filled with the fruits of the Holy Spirit: 'love, joy, peace, longsuffering, kindness, goodness, faithfulness, gentleness, self-control' (Gal 5:22–3). When the Light appears in the hearts of those born from above, the cord that binds their hearts and thoughts to the earth and its lusts is severed. Their life is now in heaven. They do not bow their heads under the Enemy's yoke and authority, or let their desires and affections run loose in any direction they please, but submit themselves to God's work and the fulfilment of His will, saying, 'I delight to do Your will, O my God' (Ps. 40:8), and 'I discipline my body and bring it into subjection' (1 Cor. 9:27). The souls illumined by the Light of God become high and lofty examples, like the righteous martyrs who sacrificed their lives, but not of the Light that embraced and reigned over them. We have likewise seen tall and shady trees, and many have gathered under the shadow provided by the branches of their righteousness. And therefore, when the Light was manifest in the world, the authority of the Angel of Darkness over the world began to fade and disappear for 'now the ruler of this world will be cast out' (John 12:31). The head and chief of darkness was deprived of all his power before all those walking the path of the Light as sons of Light and sons of the daytime. St Cyril the Great writes:

> The Word of God enlightens everyone coming into the world not by teaching the way angels, perhaps, or people do. Instead, by the divine act of creating, He inserts a seed of wisdom, or knowledge of God, and He implants a root of understanding into everything He calls into existence. In this way, He makes a living creature rational. He shows that it participates in His own nature, and He sends into the mind luminous vapours, as it were, of His ineffable brightness in a way and mode that only He Himself knows. I should not say too much about these matters I think ...

> But creation is brightened by participation with the Light,

and this is why it is called and becomes light (Matt. 5:14). It rises up above its own nature because of the grace of the One who glorifies it and who crowns it with various honours… The Lord truly 'works mercy'; things which are small and insignificant according to their own nature, He shows to be great and marvellous through His goodness toward them, just as He, as God, ungrudgingly deemed it necessary to exalt us with His own good attributes, that is why He calls us gods (cf. Jn. 10:34) and light (cf. Matt. 5:14). What good titles, after all, does He not give us?[37]

One of the Fathers meditates on the light of Christ's Resurrection thus:

> Now the sacred rays of the light of Christ shine. The pure lights of the pure Holy Spirit dawn and heavenly mysteries of glory and divinity are opened. The dark and gloomy night has been swallowed up. In this light, the pitch-black darkness has been dispelled, and the grievous shadow of death has disappeared. Life has expanded to all beings and all the universe [*tá óla*] is filled with unbounded light. The dawn of dawns has risen upon the universe [*tó pán*], and He who is 'before the morning star' (Ps 109:3 LXX), and before all the other stars, Christ, great, immortal and powerful, now shines upon all the universe more brightly than the sun. And so there is for us, who believe in Him, a new day, luminous, great and everlasting, whose light is unfading. It is the mystical Passover which was celebrated in the Law as a type but is come now to complete fullness in Christ. It is the wondrous Passover: the marvel of God's virtue and the work of God's power, the true

---

[37] Cyril of Alexandria, *Commentary on John*, I:1, 9, trans. David R. Maxwell and ed. Joel C. Elowsky (Downers Grove, IL: IVP Academic, 2013): 49–50.

feast and everlasting remembrance, passionlessness which springs out of [Christ's] Passion, immortality that springs out of death, Life that springs out of the tomb, healing that springs out of wounds, Resurrection that springs out of the fall, ascension into the heights [Heaven] that springs out of the descent [into Hades].[38]

---

[38] TN: Pseudo-Hippolytus of Rome, *On the Holy Pascha*, 1. This homily also circulated in a collection of seven Paschal homilies attributed to St John Chrysostom and for this reason it is often referred to as a Pseudo-Chrysostom's homily (cf. Pseudo-Chrysostom, *Homilies on Pascha* VI [PG 59:735–6]). For the translation from Greek, the critical text established by Pierre Nautin (*Homelies Paschales*, SC 27, (Paris: Editions du Cerf, 1950)) was used.

THE PURE IN HEART

As soon as the Lord Jesus began His famous Sermon on the Mount, the great difference between His teachings and the teachings of the Pharisees became clear. The Pharisees' teachings were coloured by hypocrisy and pretence, built around scrupulous adherence to traditions and an obligation to appear pious and godly. As for our Lord however, His teachings emphasised purity of heart. Whoever desires to belong to the Kingdom of Heaven and witness the Lord's glory must be changed from within and adorned with purity of heart for 'Blessed are the pure in heart, for they shall see God' (Matt. 5:8)

But what is *purity*? And what is meant here by *the heart*? To understand the expression 'pure in heart' we must first define both of these words according to their Greek roots, and as commonly used in the language of Holy Scripture.

'PURE'

The word *katharós* meaning *pure* is an adjective with a range of meanings in Holy Scripture.[39]

The Literal Sense: meaning clean or pure. In this sense, it refers to the essential or natural state of the thing

---

[39] *GELNT*: 388-389.

it describes. For example, the Bible speaks of a pure (i.e., clean) cup: 'first cleanse [*kathárison*] the inside of the cup and dish' (Matt. 23:26). The Bible mentions the pure linen: 'When Joseph had taken the body, he wrapped it in a clean [*kathará*] linen cloth' (Matt. 27:59); and the 'seven angels... clothed in pure [*katharón*] bright linen' (Rev. 15:6). Scripture also mentions pure water, meaning clean water suitable for use: 'Our bodies washed with pure [*katharô*] water' (Heb. 10:22).

In this sense, the Bible describes metals, such as silver and gold, as being pure and free from blemish. Thus, 'you shall also make a lampstand of pure gold' (Ex. 25:31). The word is also applied to glass or crystal in the sense of being clear or translucent: 'The construction of its wall was of jasper; and the city was pure [*katharón*] gold, like clear [*katharô*] glass... And the street of the city was pure [*katharô*] gold, like transparent glass' (Rev. 21:18, 21). When applied to bread, it means pure bread with nothing added to it: 'I am the wheat of God, and let me be ground by the teeth of the wild beasts, that I may be found the pure bread of Christ.'[40]

The Ritual Sense: meaning ritually pure, that is, permitted for use in a religious context and consequently, fit to be offered to God. This sense is frequently used in the Old Testament to describe the process of ritual purification for houses, garments and sick people (such as lepers), and is used to describe the pure foods which God permitted His people to eat. It is this ritual sense that

---

[40] Ignatius of Antioch, *Letter to the Romans* 4:1 (*ANF* 1:75).

THE PURE IN HEART

occurs in St Peter's vision: '[He] saw heaven opened… and a voice came to him, "Rise, Peter; kill and eat." But Peter said, "Not so, Lord! For I have never eaten anything common or unclean." And a voice spoke to him again the second time, "What God has cleansed you must not call common."'(Acts 10:11–15). Likewise, the Apostle Paul wrote, 'Do not destroy the work of God for the sake of food. All things indeed are pure …' (Rom. 14:20), and 'To the pure all things are pure' (Tit. 1:15).

The Moral Sense: meaning pure, clean or void of sin. This sense is generally applied to persons: 'To *the pure*, all things are pure' (Tit. 1:15); 'He who is bathed needs only to wash his feet, but *is completely clean*; and *you are clean* …' (Jn. 13:10); and '*You are already clean* because of the word which I have spoken to you' (John 15:3). This sense describes a person's physical and psychological constitution: 'In the integrity of my heart [*en kathará kardía*] and innocence of my hands I have done this' (Gen. 20:5 LXX); 'Now the purpose of the commandment is love from a pure heart [*ek katharás kardías*]' (1 Tim. 1:5); 'pursue righteousness, faith, love, peace with those who call on the Lord out of a pure heart [*ek katharás kardías*]' (2 Tim. 2:22); and 'holding the mystery of the faith with a pure conscience [*en katharás syneidései*]' (1 Tim. 3:9).

In summary, the word *katharós* describes a person or thing which is clean, having gone through a process of purification, or which is clean because it has not been mixed with anything foreign to its nature.

'THE HEART'

The word *heart*, *kardía*, also bears several meanings. In Biblical language, a person's heart is not merely the muscular organ in their chest cavity, but the centre of spiritual, natural and rational life. The heart is responsible for the following activities[41]:

The Faculty of Reason: The heart, in Holy Scripture, is responsible for our thinking processes; thoughts proceed from the heart, and it is the heart which is tasked with reason and understanding: 'out of the abundance of the heart the mouth speaks' (Matt. 12:34); 'For the hearts of this people have grown dull. Their ears are hard of hearing, and their eyes they have closed, lest they should see with their eyes and hear with their ears, lest they should understand with their hearts' (Matt. 12:34; cf. Isa. 6:10); 'Now when [Moses] was forty years old, it came into his heart to visit his brethren, the children of Israel' (Acts 7:23); 'But as it is written: "Eye has not seen, nor ear heard, nor have entered into the heart of man the things which God has prepared for those who love Him."' (1 Cor. 2:9).

Voluntary Decisions: The heart is not only in charge of our thoughts. In the Biblical understanding, the heart is also responsible for the human will and all the choices that proceed from it: 'So let each one give as he purposes in his heart, not grudgingly or of necessity; for God loves a cheerful giver' (2 Cor. 9:7); 'Therefore settle it in

---

[41] *GELNT*: 404-405.

your hearts not to meditate beforehand on what you will answer; for I will give you a mouth and wisdom…' (Lk. 21:14–15); and '[Barnabas] encouraged them all that with purpose of heart they should continue with the Lord' (Acts 11:23).

Behavioural Choices: The heart is responsible for discerning between good and evil, and for making choices between virtue and vice: 'Cleanse your hands, you sinners; and purify your hearts, you double-minded' (James 4:8); 'purifying their hearts by faith' (Acts 15:9); and 'But those things which proceed out of the mouth come from the heart, and they defile a man. For out of the heart proceed evil thoughts' (Matt. 15:18–19).

Affections, Desires and Lusts: From the heart proceed noble affections and sublime sentiments, as well as lusts and desires, whether spiritual or carnal. Behold the passionate feelings of Jeremiah the Prophet, weeping on account of those who do not know God: 'O my soul, my soul! I am pained in my very heart! My heart makes a noise in me; I cannot hold my peace' (Jer 4:19).

As for desires, the Holy Bible says, 'Therefore God also gave them up to uncleanness, in the lusts of their hearts, to dishonour their bodies among themselves" (Rom. 1:24), meaning that He had left them, taken away His help from them, so that they now followed the desires of their hearts. In addition, the Bible says, 'whoever looks at a woman to lust for her has already committed adultery with her in his heart' (Matt. 5:28).

From these many uses of these two words (purity and heart) in Holy Scripture, we can come to understand some of the meanings that our Lord Jesus intended when He said to His disciples, 'Blessed are the pure in heart.'

The pure in heart to whom the Lord refers here are those who have set themselves up to be perfectly pure of any blemish that does not accord with God's nature. They have subjected their thoughts, their wills, their moral principles, and their emotions — that is, every aspect of their human personality — to a process of strict and comprehensive purification and cleansing, through the action of the Holy Spirit within them.

The pure in heart are also the elect, chosen on account of their faithful fulfilment of God's will and walking in His ways, who never gave themselves the right to be ruled by any master or god except the Lord God. They are the ones chosen to serve the Kingdom of God, worthy of beholding His glory.

In the Beatitudes, the Lord Jesus indicated that the pure in heart shall see God. This notion was of the utmost importance for the children of Israel, for they knew that Moses had seen the Lord face to face (cf. Ex. 33:11), and that King David had asked God to grant him a pure heart so that the Holy Spirit might dwell within him (cf. Ps. 51:10, 11), and that Isaiah the Prophet had been found worthy to enter the Holies on high and to see God (cf. Isa. 6:5). Thus, the disciples and the multitudes who heard the Lord's sermon longed to be in the

THE PURE IN HEART

presence of God, or put another way, to behold the glory of God, as it was beheld by their great prophets. This is what the disciples expressed by the mouth of Philip: 'Lord, show us the Father, and it is sufficient for us' (John 14:8).

The children of Israel also seemed to realise that there are necessary foundations which anyone who wants to see God must acquire. The Psalmist asked what the requirements are to be in God's presence when he posed his question: 'Who may ascend into the hill of the Lord? Or who may stand in His holy place?' (Ps 24:3) The answer he gives is: 'He who has clean hands and a pure heart, who has not lifted up his soul to an idol, nor sworn deceitfully' (Ps. 24:4). Thus, outward cleanness and inward purity both refer to the state of holiness required of those who are called to appear in the presence of God. It was this same calling which the Lord Jesus extended to his listeners that as the children of the promises and heirs of the Torah, they knew the conditions required for being in the presence of God. This, the Lord Jesus summed up in a single condition, comprising all the notions of inward and outward purity, that is, the purity of heart.

This call for purity would not have been strange to the ears of anyone who was well-versed in the Torah and kept its commandments. But even so, it represented a powerful challenge to the requirements of righteousness cried up by the teachers of the Law and the Pharisees. Their teachings focused on the outward appearance of righteousness, which the Lord described when He said: 'Woe to you, scribes and Pharisees, hypocrites! For you cleanse the outside of the cup and dish, but inside they are full of extortion and self-indulgence' (Matt. 23:25). When one dresses up their lives with hypocrisy and false outward piety, one may appear to be pure before the congregation, but how far one is from beholding the Lord's glory and seeing His face!

The Pharisee stood up, completely adorned with false works of righteousness, and began to recite his virtues before God: 'I fast twice a week; I give tithes of all that I possess' (Luke 18:12). But he went out from the Lord's presence condemned, not justified. This is why the Lord Jesus' teachings to His disciples focused on the inward parts; He gave them the key through which they would be able to see the glory of God, which is the purity of heart.

Who, then, are the pure in heart, who have open eyes, and who are capable of beholding the glory of the Lord?

They are those who have readied themselves to undergo a process of inward purification. Just as the word (*katharós*) in Scripture means 'clean after washing, ritually pure, pure from all blemish', purity of heart is not something passive, it is not just the opposite of impurity; it is rather an active state, one that demands willpower, work and total surrender and submission to the Holy Spirit. The disciple of Christ must come to Him daily, confessing his shortcomings so that the Lord might purify him continually:

> Therefore, brethren, having boldness to enter the Holiest by the blood of Jesus... let us draw near with *a true heart* in full assurance of faith, having our hearts sprinkled from an evil conscience and our bodies washed with pure water (Heb. 10:19–22).

He must also fill his heart every day with longing for the Lord, so that no place remains in his heart for anything foreign:

> That he would grant you, according to the riches of his glory, to be strengthened with might through His Spirit in the inner man, that Christ may dwell in your hearts through faith... that you may be filled with all the fullness of God (Eph. 3:16–19).

The follower of Christ must keep watch, guarding his heart from the enticement of evil desires: 'Keep your heart with all diligence, for out of it spring the issues of life' (Prov. 4:23).

As gold goes through several stages of purification before all its impurities are cleansed and it becomes pure, furnace-refined gold, so it is with the disciple of the Lord: his inward parts must be purified from all blemishes and become a pure heart capable of beholding the glory of the Lord.

The pure in heart are those whose hearts are clear and transparent. Just as the word *pure* (*katharós*) is used to describe clear and transparent things like glass or crystal, things we can see through easily without any obscurity, so also the pure in heart are those who enjoy sincerity and transparency before God, such that they hide nothing from His eyes.

Of course, we cannot hide anything from God's eyes, for, as the Psalmist says, 'He knows the secrets of the heart' (Ps. 44:21). But in our weakness, we many times try to conceal parts of ourselves so that they can be ruled by another master, whether a carnal lust or desire of the soul. But those with pure, clear and transparent hearts uncover their entire selves before God so that He might use them for the glory of His name.

Blessed are those who have given themselves up completely before the Lord's eyes, for when they stand in His presence, they will see Him face to face: 'But we all, with unveiled face, beholding as in a mirror the glory of the Lord, are being transformed into the same image from glory to glory, just as by the Spirit of the Lord' (2 Cor. 3:18).

The pure in heart are those who possess a whole and undivided heart. Just as the word heart (*kardía*) in Holy Scripture refers to the whole human being, including the will, desires and emotions, so the pure in heart are those who have surrendered this whole and entire heart to the Lord, and become worthy of beholding His glory: 'And you shall love the Lord your God with all your heart, with all your soul, with all your mind, and with all your strength' (Mark 12:30). When the rich young man approached the Lord Jesus asking, 'What shall I do that I may inherit eternal life? (Mark 10:17), the Lord's

THE PURE IN HEART

answer was the he ought to sell all he had and give to the poor, then come and follow Him (cf. Mark 10:21). For the Lord saw that the love of money reigned in this young man's heart, and that it stood in the way of his inheriting eternal life, as the Biblical account makes clear when it says, 'He was sad at this word, and went away sorrowful, for he had great possessions' (Mark 10:22). The chief thing this youth needed to do to become worthy of inheriting the Kingdom was to sell all his possessions and give to the poor. Perhaps if the Lord Jesus had said to him 'Come and follow me!' the youth would have—to all appearances—agreed and taken up the offer. But he would never have been able to endure hearing the Lord say, 'Foxes have holes and birds of the air have nests, but the Son of Man has nowhere to lay His head' (Luke 9:58). The pure in heart are those who have surrendered their *whole* hearts to God, not just *most* of their hearts. The Lord commanded, 'My son, give me your heart, and let your eyes observe my ways' (Prov. 23:26). If we give Him our whole heart, our eyes will be opened and we will see and behold His way and His will toward us.

CHILDREN OF ABRAHAM

The name of Abraham, the father of fathers, is repeated many times in the New Testament. In John's Gospel alone, it appears eleven times, all of them in the eighth chapter (v. 31–58). Knowing how the Jews in the days of Christ viewed their connection to Abraham will help us better understand the conversation between Christ and the Jews in this chapter.

God had blessed Abraham and given him this promise:

> I will make you a great nation; I will bless you and make your name great; and you shall be a blessing. I will bless those who bless you, and I will curse him who curses you; and in you all the families of the earth shall be blessed (Gen. 12:2–3).

God also added to this promise, saying: 'To your descendants I will give this land' (Gen. 12:7). This promise was then confirmed for Abraham when God promised the birth of Isaac: '"Look now toward heaven, and count the stars if you are able to number them." And He said to him, "So shall your descendants be."' (Gen. 15:1–6). The promise was confirmed again when God changed Abraham's name from Abram (*'Avrām*) to Abraham (*'Avrāhām*) of which circumcision was a sign of the promise (cf. Gen. 17:1–14).

This was the Biblical basis for the high esteem in which the character of Abraham was held in later Jewish tradition, on account of his mighty feats and his exemplary character.[42] The Jews poured streams of praise upon Abraham because he had fulfilled the strictest demands of the virtuous life, the sort of life lauded among the Greek philosophers. The Jewish historian Josephus describes him as 'a man in every virtue supreme.'[43] The Mishnah, a collection of teachings of Jewish Rabbis referred to in the Gospels as 'the tradition of the elders' (Mk. 7:3), comments on the verse from Genesis which says, 'Because Abraham obeyed My voice and kept My charge, My commandments, My statutes, and My laws' (Gen. 25:6), stating, 'Abraham our father had performed the whole Law before it was given.'[44] The Mishnah likewise considers him the first man to condemn the worship of idols, because of his faith in God. Indeed, Josephus tells us that the only reason Abraham left the region between the two rivers was the enmity he endured because he refused to worship idols.[45]

Because of this great honour bestowed on Abraham, wonderful tales were told about him. These tales are

---

[42] Cf. Joachim Jeremias, 'Abram', *TDNT*, I: 8.

[43] Josephus, *Antiquities of the Jews*, I:256. Cf. *Josephus*, Vol. 4, trans. H. St. J. Thackeray (London: William Heinemann, 1956): 127.

[44] Mishnah, *Kiddushin* 4:14 (cf. *Mishnah*: 329).

[45] Cf. Josephus, *Antiquities of the Jews*, I:154-157. Cf. *Josephus*, Vol. 4, trans. H. St. J. Thackeray (London: William Heinemann, 1956): 77-79.

CHILDREN OF ABRAHAM

recorded in late Jewish texts like *The Apocalypse of Abraham* and *The Testament of Abraham* which cover the history of Abraham's life as given in Genesis, with the addition of Rabbinic legends describing his interactions with angels, visions in which he saw God, and journeys he had to the heavenly realm[46].

Yet the highest praise given to Abraham is found in the Jewish tradition which holds that Abraham's faith and obedience—along with the righteousness of Isaac and Jacob—were so great, and such an immense treasure, that they are referred to collectively as 'the merits of the fathers'.[47] This treasury of the patriarchs' righteousness and holiness surpassed what was needed for them to attain salvation, and so it was believed that God allowed this righteousness to be transferred to any Jewish person who needed to atone for his sins. Even though some

---

[46] Cf. Emil Schürer, *The History of the Jewish People in the Age of Jesus Christ*, III.2 (Edinburgh: T&T Clark Ltd, 1987): 761.

[47] TN: This is a reference to the Rabbinic notion of $z^ekût\ ab\hat{o}t$, whereby Israel can find favour with God by appealing to the righteousness of their forefathers Abraham, Isaac and Jacob. The first Biblical instance of this occurs in Ex. 32:13. See Joshua H Shmidman, 'Zekhut Avot', *Encyclopaedia Judaica*, ed. M. Berenbaum and F. Skolnik, 2nd edn, vol. 21 (Macmillan, 2007): 497–498 and Arthuer Marmorstein, *The Doctrine of Merits in Old Rabbinical Literature* (New York: Ktav, 1968). Hints of this concept survive in the prayers of the Coptic Church; for instance, in the ninth hour troparia of the Agpia (Horologion) we find a plea for mercy 'for the sake of Your beloved Abraham, Your servant Isaac, and Israel Your saint' (cf. Daniel 3:35 LXX).

Rabbis opposed this view, its existence is a testament to the great honour which Abraham had attained.[48]

The people of Israel were the descendants of Abraham, and therefore, they were the chosen people in whom the promises and blessings of God granted to Abraham were fulfilled. Yet none of these promises or blessings were to be fulfilled except in the Messiah who was to come from Abraham's line. For this reason, Jewish writings always refer to Abraham as 'our father Abraham'. This is the very title we find on the pages of the New Testament:

> The oath which He swore to our father Abraham: to grant us that we, being delivered from the hand of our enemies, might serve Him without fear (Luke 1:73–4).

> The God of glory appeared to our father Abraham when he was in Mesopotamia, before he dwelt in Haran (Acts 7:2).

> What then shall we say that Abraham our father has found according to the flesh?... and the father of circumcision to those who not only are of the circumcision, but who also walk in the steps of the faith which our father Abraham had while still uncircumcised (Rom. 4:1, 12).

> Was not Abraham our father justified by works when he offered Isaac his son on the altar? (James 2:21).

The Lord Jesus Himself used this term of address in the parable of Lazarus and the rich man, for He says (in

---

[48] Cf. Harold S. Songer, 'Sons of Abraham', *Biblical Illustrator*, Winter 94: 61–4.

CHILDREN OF ABRAHAM

the character of the rich man who has gone down to Hades): 'Father Abraham, have mercy on me, and send Lazarus that he may dip the tip of his finger in water and cool my tongue' (Luke 16:19–31). Thus, the Jews were commonly called 'the children of Abraham' (John 8:39) or 'Abraham's descendants' (John 8:33), and an individual Jew could be called 'a son of Abraham' (Luke 19:9) or 'a daughter of Abraham' (Luke 13:16).

These frequent allusions to Abraham as a father to the Jews and the designation of the Jews as Abraham's descendants call for a precise investigation, for it is possible that they have a meaning entirely different to the intended one. Does this title indicate some sort of special distinction, privilege or worthiness belonging to the Jews, or does it rather point to the duties and obligations laid upon anyone who bears it?

Both of these meanings—privilege and duty—are clearly present in the Genesis account. The promises granted to Abraham in the Book of Genesis are tied to his faith and obedience. The promise of blessing in Genesis 18 is linked to God's command to Abraham, 'Get out of your country, from your family and from your father's house, to a land that I will show you' (Gen. 12:1). Likewise, when the promise is confirmed and a further promise to grant Abraham the inheritance of the earth, both elements are necessarily included: gift and obligation. The promise of the birth of an heir demands faith (cf. Gen 15:1–6), and the promise to inherit the earth requires the offering of a sacrifice (cf. Gen 15:7–21). The confirmation of the promise through the sign of circumcision (cf. Gen 17:2–14) is preceded by the commandment: 'I am Almighty God; walk before Me and be blameless' (Gen. 17:1).

Even after God had granted him Isaac and sworn that Abraham would become the heir of the promises and blessings, a test of faith was required to confirm God's promise and blessing, for God asked Abraham to offer up Isaac as a sacrifice. And the test was whether Abraham believed that God could raise Isaac from the dead—Isaac, in whom he had received the promises, his only son (cf. Gen. 22:1–18).

At the time of Christ's incarnation, we find both these notions—special distinction and obligation—in the being descendants of Abraham. However, at the time, the Jews placed more emphasis on the notion of special distinction and honour, with little attention given to the requirements that accompany this sonship. In the sayings of the Jewish Rabbis of that era, being a child of Abraham was described as an absolute right, not contingent on any conditions. Thus, Rabbi Meir said that even though the Jews are full of blemishes (cf. Deut. 32:5), even though the children deal corruptly (cf. Isa. 1:4), and even though they are wise to do evil (cf. Jer. 4:22), still they are called "sons."[49]

---

[49] *Sifre on Deuteronomy*, 308. Cf. Reuven Hammer (ed.), *Sifre: A Tannaitic Commentary on the Book of Deuteronomy* (New Haven, CT, Yale University Press, 1986): 313.

CHILDREN OF ABRAHAM

This way of thinking was widespread in the time of Christ. The Jewish people thought that so long as they were children of Abraham, they had the right to inherit the promises, inherit the earth, and a glorious future. In his *Dialogue with Trypho*, St Justin Martyr reports that the Jews, as Abraham's children, expected to reap the rewards of the Kingdom of God regardless of their manner of life.[50] St John the Baptist confronted this erroneous idea when the Jews first began to accept his call to repentance:

> Then he said to the multitudes that came out to be baptized by him, 'Brood of vipers! Who warned you to flee from the wrath to come? Therefore bear fruits worthy of repentance, and do not begin to say to yourselves, "We have Abraham as our father." For I say to you that God is able to raise up children to Abraham from these stones. And even now the axe is laid to the root of the trees. Therefore, every tree which does not bear good fruit is cut down and thrown into the fire' (Luke 3:7–9).

John is here reminding those listening to him that being a child of Abraham does not void the command of God to every human being: 'Walk before Me and be blameless' (Gen. 17:1).

There were, however, some more moderate Rabbis who understood being a child of Abraham as a matter of duty and responsibility to fulfil its demands. These Rabbis preached that it was necessary to emulate the morals

---

[50] Cf. Justin Martyr, *Dialogue with Trypho*, 140:2 (PG 6:797) (ANF 1:269).

and virtues of Abraham. In the Mishnah, we find the following notion:

> He in whom are these three things is of the disciples of Abraham our father; but [he in whom are] three other things is of the disciples of Balaam the wicked. A good eye and a humble spirit and a lowly [*sanctified*] soul—[they in whom are these] are of the disciples of Abraham our father. An evil eye, a haughty spirit, a proud soul— [they in whom are these] are of the disciples of Balaam the wicked… The disciples of Abraham our father enjoy this world and inherit the world to come… The disciples of Balaam the wicked inherit Gehenna and go down to the pit of destruction.[51]

This passage from the teachings of the Rabbis shows that there were some among Israel's spiritual leaders who held that it was a man's spiritual conduct that determined his fate, and not simply his belonging to the seed of Abraham. The Lord Jesus endorsed this concept during His encounter with Zacchaeus the chief tax collector. After Zacchaeus had declared his repentance and committed to have compassion on the poor and oppressed, and to cease the wicked works he had been doing, the Lord Jesus answered him saying, 'Today salvation has come to this house, because he also is a son of Abraham' (Luke 19:9). St Paul also affirmed this concept in his letters, for his teachings declare that in Christ there is no spiritual significance to a person's roots, whether they be Jew or Gentile (cf. Gal. 3:28), and that a person

---

[51] *Pirqê avôt* 5:19. Cf. *Mishnah*: 458.

should not be accounted a Jew if he is only a Jew outwardly, that is, simply because he belongs to the seed of Abraham, and that circumcision should not be considered circumcision if it is only carried out in the flesh. According to St Paul, a true Jew is a Jew inwardly, that is, one who follows in the footsteps of Abraham's faith (cf. Rom. 2:28–29).

We can now better examine the conversation between the Lord Jesus and the Jews in the eighth chapter of John's Gospel. When the Lord Jesus informed the Jews of their need for freedom— 'and you shall know the truth, and the truth shall make you free' (John 8:32)—they responded from the Rabbinic perspective which emphasises the privilege and distinction of the descent from Abraham, saying, 'We are Abraham's descendants, and have never been in bondage to anyone' (John 8:33). This is the view which considers all Jews free, though at that time, they were enslaved under the Roman state. Rabbi Akiva said, 'Even the poorest in Israel are looked upon as freemen who have lost their possessions, for they are the sons of Abraham, Isaac and Jacob.'[52]

The Lord Jesus awakened in these Jews—who seemed at first to accept Christ's words—thoughts that had been buried and cemented over centuries and generations, resting on a fanatical, political nationalism tinged with outward piousness, emblazoned with the slogan of "YHWH"; a sacred, inviolable politics. They

---

[52] Mishnà Baba Kamma 8:6 (Mishnah: 343).

must have thought how could this teacher deny their freedom when they have received dominion over all the peoples and nations of the world through God's promise to their father Abraham? If their land and nation had been invaded by hostile armies over the centuries—Egyptians, Babylonians, Assyrians and Romans—still, they all departed just as they came, without violating their heritage, inheritance, customs or worship. The Jews came out from under the yoke of bondage as free as they had ever been, in the promise of their father Abraham. How then could this man promise them freedom when they already stood free?[53]

The Lord Jesus had no qualms about their fleshly descent from Abraham: 'I know that you are Abraham's descendants' (John 8:37). But He added that they had another father: 'I speak what I have seen with My Father, and you do what you have seen with your father' (8:38). With these words, He was provoking them to assert their claim to be children of Abraham: 'They answered and said to Him, "Abraham is our father."' (8:39) And here the Lord refutes their claim, appealing to the Jewish teaching which holds that the true children of Abraham are the righteous. By comparing Abraham's deeds to theirs, He demonstrates that they are not Abraham's children: 'If you were Abraham's children, you would do the works of Abraham. But now you seek to kill Me, a Man who has told you the truth which I heard from

---

[53] Cf. Mattā al-Miskīn, *Šarḥ ingīl al-qiddīs yūḥannā*, I (Wādī al-Naṭrūn, Monastery of St Macarius, 1990): 544

CHILDREN OF ABRAHAM

God. Abraham did not do this' (8:39–40). That is to say, Abraham was no murderer, but you want to murder Me; Abraham did not resist the truth, but you fight against Me because I spoke the truth to you; Abraham was obedient to the words of God, but you resist the words which I have told you I received from God.

Thus, Christ tells the Jews that Abraham received the messengers God sent to him, made them his guests and heeded their words, but you reject 'Him whom the Father sanctified and sent into the world' (John 10:36). The works which they did, Abraham did not do. Therefore, their descent from Abraham profited them nothing.

At this point, the Jews realised that they had taken the bait He had set out for them; He had bested them in this round. So, they abandoned their insistence that they were children of Abraham and claimed instead that they had no father except God, saying, 'We have one Father—God' (John 8:41), relying upon a prophecy of Isaiah's: 'You are our Father, though Abraham was ignorant of us, and Israel does not acknowledge us. You, O Lord, are our Father; Our Redeemer from Everlasting is Your name' (Isa. 63:16).

Here, the Lord Jesus vigorously refuted their claim to be children of God. To be a child of God also brings with it many duties and requirements. Perhaps the Lord Jesus was also referring to a prophecy of Isaiah's: 'I have nourished and brought up children, and they have rebelled against Me... Alas, sinful nation, a people laden with iniquity, a brood of evildoers [*and not children of*

God], children who are corrupters!' (Isa. 1:2–4). From what the Lord Jesus saw before Him, these men were not children of God, but had another father, the Devil. 'You are of your father the devil, and the desires of your father you want to do. He was a murderer from the beginning, and does not stand in the truth, because there is no truth in him. When he speaks a lie, he speaks from his own resources, for he is a liar and the father of it' (John 8:44). In this accusation, the Lord Jesus was once again referring to a prophecy from Isaiah: 'Are you not children of transgression, offspring of falsehood?' (Isa. 57:4).

The Lord Jesus wanted to affirm that mere biological descent from Abraham will profit a man nothing if the person does not also walk in the footsteps of Abraham:

> Many will come from east and west, and sit down with Abraham, Isaac, and Jacob in the Kingdom of Heaven. But the sons of the kingdom will be cast out into outer darkness (Matt. 8:11–12).

Even our claim to belong to God does not suffice because God will deny it if we do not keep its requirements: 'Depart from Me, you who practice lawlessness. I never knew you!' (Matt. 7:23). But if we do the will of God, not only will we become children to Him, but Christ will call us 'My brother, My sister and My mother' (Matt. 12:5).

SEEK THE LORD

In the middle of the eighth century before Christ's birth, the northern kingdom of Israel was in a state of social, political and religious anarchy. These three aspects of life were then, as now, intricately bound up with each other. The social and political problems in the days of the prophet Amos had a clear effect on religious life. The chief reason for the worsening of the religious problems at this time were due to the hopes and dreams that the nation and its citizens were seeking after.

The words that the prophet Amos wrote about this nation were a message from the Lord of Israel. They were not the words of a human being, but of the mighty Lord who openly declared Himself as such, saying, 'For thus says the Lord to the house of Israel: "Seek me and live!"' (Amos 5:4).

The Hebrew word translated here as 'the Lord' is 'YHWH', the personal name of God. In the book of Exodus (3:14–15) God identifies Himself to Moses with this name; when Moses asked what name he should report to the children of Israel, God answered him: '*Ehyeh 'ăšer 'ehyeh*' or 'I Am Who I Am' or 'I Am the Self-Existent' or, as the Lord Jesus says in the New Testament, 'I Am' (John 8:58). Whatever the literal meaning of this name, it was the name the children of Israel used to identify the God they worshipped as distinct from the many pagan gods who were widely worshipped in the Ancient Near East. For this reason, God declared His individuality and oneness to the children of Israel at the beginning of the commandments He gave to His people, known as the $š^ema'$ ('hear'): 'Hear O Israel: the Lord our God is one' (Deut. 6:4). The word 'one' in this commandment signifies unity and individuality. The meaning is clear: God is one; there is no God apart from Him.

'Seek the Lord' is the message of many prophets throughout the ages. But what did the phrase 'seek the Lord' mean in the days of Amos the prophet?

The verb here translated as 'seek' is the Hebrew *dāraš*. This word means more than merely to seek. It means to seek with care and diligence, to consult a prophet, priest, or seer for a decision or the answer to a question. One who seeks in this way is searching for a divine solution to his or her problem, and it requires great diligence from the seeker. So *seeking* here implies a seeking directed towards God, persistence in turning to Him, and in doing this always, as a way of life. To seek God and search for Him means to live a life in submission to His will, moving in accordance with His direction. A people that seek God will conduct all their transactions with justice and righteousness, and God will be their guide in all that they do. In short, to seek the Lord is to do His will.[54]

---

[54] Cf. Robert Laird Harris, *Theological Wordbook of the Old Testament*, (Chicago: Moody Press, 1980), I: 198.

SEEK THE LORD

The Lord commanded His people by the mouth of Amos the prophet: 'Seek Me and live; but do not seek Bethel, nor enter Gilgal, nor pass over to Beersheba' (Amos 5:4–5). Bethel, Gilgal and Beersheba are set forth here as substitutes for seeking God. Bethel and Gilgal were well-known holy places in the northern kingdom of Israel. It was Abraham, the father of fathers, who established Bethel (cf. Gen. 12:8, 13:3–4), and Gilgal had been associated with Hebrew worship since the days of Joshua the son of Nun (cf. Josh. 4:19–24) and throughout the reign of the Judges (cf. Judg. 2). Beersheba lay on the southern border of the kingdom of Judah, about 64 kilometres south of Jerusalem, and was also connected with Abraham the father of fathers (cf. Gen. 21:25–33). These three locations represented holy places used for worship over many centuries, continuing into the days of Amos.

The prophet Amos, speaking in God's name, commanded the people to stop consulting priests and astrologers in these three places and instead to seek God alone. The words of Amos reveal the sorts of practices that were performed in the name of YHWH in these places, but which were rejected by God. The religious fervour found in Bethel and Gilgal—for all its religious character—was considered a kind of disobedience and rebellion against God. In their attempt to display their own personal righteousness, the people were trying to offer more than was required of them in the Law:

'Come to Bethel and transgress, at Gilgal multiply

transgression; bring your sacrifices every morning, your tithes every three days. Offer a sacrifice of thanksgiving with leaven, proclaim and announce the freewill offerings; for this you love, You children of Israel!' says the Lord God (Amos 4:4-6).

The Lord therefore declared His rejection of these religious practices by the mouth of the prophet Amos, even though they were performed in the name of the Lord:

> I hate, I despise your feast days, and I do not savour your sacred assemblies. Though you offer Me burnt offerings and your grain offerings, I will not accept them, nor will I regard your fattened peace offerings. Take away from Me the noise of your songs, for I will not hear the melody of your stringed instruments (Amos 5:21–3).

The worship of God had become a kind of mechanical worship, empty of spirit. Concern for rites and hymns had taken the place of a living, personal connection with God. For this reason, Amos cried out to the people, imploring them to put an end to their external displays of worship and instead turn to the worship of God from the heart. God declared His will for the people with these words: 'Let justice run down like water, and righteousness like a mighty stream' (Amos 5:24).

The prophet then went back to explain further what was meant by seeking the Lord in his saying: 'Seek good and not evil, that you may live' (Amos 5:14). Here, the prophet is setting up a comparison. He compares seeking the Lord to seeking good, and seeking evil to seeking Bethel, Gilgal and Beersheba. Even though these places were revered as holy and sacred to the worship of God, God rejected this worship because it was not true worship. It was merely a formal kind of worship; what was sought in this worship was not the face of God, but the completion of outward and empty ordinances and rituals.

This bleak picture is not far removed from us today. There are some who think that merely going to Church, completing the rites, and paying one's tithes and vows is all that is necessary in worship. In ancient times, Amos exhorted the people to enter into a personal relationship with God, and not to perform the rites in a purely formal manner, because although rites in themselves were required, what was necessary was true worship. The Lord Jesus rebuked the scribes and Pharisees who tithed mint and anise and cumin, but neglected the weightier things of the law: 'Justice and mercy and faith' (Matt. 23:23). They took great care to keep the teachings of the Law and the Temple which directed them to give a tithe of everything they acquired; in this respect, they did not sin. Their sin was rather that they formally fulfilled God's commandments without piercing through into the essence of God's commandment: 'I desire mercy and not sacrifice' (Matt. 9:13).

It is strange that a people like this, so far from God, seeking after the form of worship disconnected from its essence, was eager for the day of the Lord: 'Woe to you who desire the day of the Lord!' (Amos 5:18). They were expecting the day of the Lord would come to them in righteousness, bringing about the judgement of Israel's enemies and restoring Israel to her exalted place among the surrounding nations. Perhaps they supposed that the Lord's day would be a day of worship to the Lord, in which they would offer pure worship from their hearts; in modern terms, they thought the day of the Lord was 'the solution'.

But regardless of their views on the day of the Lord, the prophet Amos had a very different perspective on the Lord's day; he declared that it would be a day of darkness, not light (cf. Amos 5:18) and that the judgement of the Lord would not be what they were expecting. Amos was speaking of the condemnation God would bring against Israel. The day of the Lord was not, for Amos, a day yet to come, but a day present among them. And the prophet's outlook was not grim or pessimistic, but filled with hope: 'Seek the Lord and live'. The foundation of seeking the Lord is the life of repentance and change—change in the sense of responding to the Lord's judgement, the change of one's manner of life to bring it into accordance with God's will. This change will manifest itself in the establishment of justice on earth, and mercy and faithfulness in people's lives. Such a transformation will have a direct effect on the religious, political and social life of the people.

The day of the Lord is not a future day but a present one; a day we live and feel every day. The day of the Lord comes upon us every day in which we hear His

SEEK THE LORD

word and feel His presence! It comes upon us every day that we approach His holy table and unite with Him. This is the day of the Lord, and this is the prophet's call for us: that we should seek the Lord, that our hearts might live, that we should be united with Him, and live with Him and through Him.

THE TRANSFIGURATION OF CHRIST AND THE TRANSFIGURATION OF THE DISCIPLES

While the Lord Jesus was in the company of His disciples near Caesarea Philippi (the modern city of Bāniyās) on the slopes of Mount Hermon, He asked them, 'Who do men say that I am?' (Mark 8:27). After they offered answers which showed the people's confusion and differing opinions, He asked them directly, 'But you, who do you say that I am?' (Mark 8,29). And here the disciples confess through the mouth of the Apostle Peter: 'You are the Christ, the Son of the living God' (Matt. 16:16).

He then revealed to them that the Son of Man would come into the glory of His Father with His angels, and that some of them would not taste death before they would see the Son of Man coming in His kingdom. It was six days after this conversation that He took His three closest disciples—Peter, James and John—and went up to a high mountain with them alone. There, His form was changed before them for His face shone like the sun and His garments became white as the light. Then Moses and Elijah appeared to them, speaking with the Lord, and as the disciples were unable to bear this sight, they fell on their faces in fear (cf. Matt. 17:1–8).

ANBA EPIPHANIUS

The Gospel writers expressed the concept of 'transfiguration' with the Greek verb *metamorphóomai*. This word is formed from two parts: the first, *meta-*, denotes a change, shift or transformation; the second is derived from the word *morphḗ* and means 'outward expression proceeding from and being truly representative of one's inward character and nature'[55] Thus, the meaning of the verb is: 'his outward expression was changed… which outward expression proceeded from and was truly representative of his inward being.'[56] Therefore, this word in Arabic has been translated 'His appearance was changed'.

Throughout His life on earth, the Lord Jesus was in the form of a slave, with no form or beauty that we should desire Him, despised and rejected by men (cf. Isa. 53:2). For He did not come to be served, but to serve, and to give His life a ransom for many (cf. Mark 10:45). But here, on the Mount of Transfiguration, His appearance and outward form was changed; He appeared in the image of the glory of His divinity. This is the sense implied by the Greek verb *metamorphóomai*. The Lord changed His outward appearance—that is, the form of a slave which He had assumed for Himself—so that His outward form became a perfect expression of His

---

[55] Cf. Kenneth S. Wuest, *Studies in the Vocabulary of the Greek New Testament*, (Grand Rapids, MI: Wm. B. Eerdmans Publishing Co., 1945): 49–50.

[56] *Ibid.*: 51.

THE TRANSFIGURATION OF CHRIST...

internal reality, an expression, that is, of divinity manifested in the body.

To understand better the kind of change that took place, let us compare the Greek verb *metamorphóomai* with another verb, which also is translates 'to change'.

In the second letter to the Corinthians (11:13–5), St Paul says, 'For such are false apostles, deceitful workers, transforming themselves into apostles of Christ. And no wonder! For Satan himself transforms himself [*metaschēmatízetai*] into an angel of light' (2 Cor. 11:13-14). The Greek verb used in this verse also is formed of two parts. The first is the same prefix used in the previous word, i.e. *meta-*, which indicates a change or transformation; the second derives from the word *schēma*, which is also translated form or appearance. However, the meaning of the verb here is completely opposite to the previous one; we might render its meaning: 'to change one's external appearance or image, so that one's form or external image does not reflect or express one's internal character.'[57]

The meaning of this verb is best captured in the word 'to disguise', i.e. to wear a face or mask as a disguise, concealing one's appearance. Satan's nature is dark; when he appears as an angel of light, it is only his outward appearance that changes. His dark nature remains entirely unchanged. Likewise, his servants change their

---

[57] St Paul uses this verb with its positive meaning once in his letter to the Philippians (3:21): 'Who will transform [*metaschēmatísei*] our lowly body that it may be conformed to His glorious body.'

outward form to resemble apostles of Christ, but in their inner nature they still remain the same deceitful workers, because they deceive the hearts of the simple. So whereas the first verb (*metamorphóomai*) indicates a change which reflects the *inner* reality, the second one (*metaschēmatízetai*) indicates an *external* one.[58]

The Lord's transfiguration on the Mount of Transfiguration and His appearance in the form of His glory can be better understood from the doxology that St Paul delivered in his letter to the Philippians. This doxology explains how the Lord Jesus, being in the form of God, took to Himself the form of the slave to bring about that slave's redemption:

> Let this mind be in you which was also in Christ Jesus,
> who, being in the form of God,
> did not consider it robbery
> to be equal with God,
> but made Himself of no reputation,
> taking the form of a bondservant,
> and coming in the likeness of men.
> And being found in appearance as a man,
> He humbled Himself
> and became obedient to the point of death,
> even the death of the Cross.
> Therefore God also has highly exalted Him
> and given Him the name
> which is above every name,

---

[58] Cf. W. E. Vine, *Vine's Complete Expository Dictionary of Old and New Testament Words* (Nashville, TN: Thomas Nelson Publishers, 1985): 639.

that at the name of Jesus every knee should bow,
of those in heaven, and of those on earth,
and of those under the earth,
and that every tongue should confess
that Jesus Christ is Lord,
to the glory of God the Father (Phil. 2:5–11).

The Transfiguration of the Saints

St Peter the Apostle spoke of the transfiguration of the Lord Jesus on the mountain and His appearing in His true glorious form, describing this glory in exalted terms:

> We made known to you the power and coming of our Lord Jesus Christ, but we were eyewitnesses of His majesty. For He received from God the Father honour and glory when such a voice came to Him from the Excellent Glory: 'This is My beloved Son, in whom I am well pleased.' And we heard this voice which came from heaven when we were with Him on the holy mountain (2 Pet. 1:16–18).

The Apostle Paul, moreover, exhorts all believers to be changed, to undergo a transfiguration like that of the Lord Jesus. In his let-er to the Romans, he implores the believers, 'Do not be conformed [*synschēmatízesthe*] to this world, but be transformed by the renewing of your mind, that you may prove what is that good and acceptable and perfect will of God' (Rom. 12:2).

In this verse, St Paul uses both verbs we have just discussed. The first verb—'Do not be conformed'—is the same as that used in 2 Corinthians 11:15 to describe the devil who changes his form into the likeness of an angel of light. Here, St Paul is urging the believers not to be *con*-formed to this age, that is, not to be of the same kind; not to be outwardly transformed into an image that does not flow from or reflect their inner nature. He commands them not to disguise themselves beneath the outward appearance of the children of this age, which does not reflect the new man which was created according to God, in true righteousness and holiness (Eph. 4:24).[59]

In the rest of the verse, he commands them to be *trans*-formed, and here he used the same verb that is found in the account of the Transfiguration. Here, he is commanding the believers to be transfigured, to reveal through their outward conduct the new, true nature in which they now live. This outward conduct reveals the image of Christ imprinted upon their hearts: 'My little children, for whom I labour in birth again until Christ is formed in you' (Gal. 4:19).

St Paul's command to the saints of Corinth to be transformed—that is, transfigured—is supported by the important truth that in the future resurrection, the saints will undergo a transfiguration. Their outward appearance will become an expression of the new nature they will have inherited when their bodies are conformed to

---

[59] Cf. Kenneth S. Wuest, *Golden Nuggets from the Greek New Testament* (Grand Rapids, MI: William B. Eerdmans Publishing Company, 1945): 26–28.

the image of His glorious body.[60] Thus, in 2 Corinthians (3:18), St Paul says:

> But we all, with unveiled face, beholding as in a mirror the glory of the Lord, are being transformed [*metamorfoúmetha*] into the same image from glory to glory, just as by the Lord the Spirit.[61]

Here, St Paul used the same verb used to describe the Transfiguration, but the transfiguration in this case shall be into the image of the Word, when the image of God is impressed upon our faces; a transformation or transfiguration shall take place in our nature, though in a dynamic and continuous movement that never ceases 'from glory to glory' (cf. 2 Cor. 3:18) by the power of the working of the Lord's Spirit within us.

---

[60] TN: An implicit reference to Phil 3:21: '…who will transform our lowly body that it may be conformed to His glorious body.'

[61] TN: Translation is ours to match the Arabic.

HOSANNA TO THE SON OF DAVID

An important source for the Greek word Hosanna is in Psalm 118, verse 25, where the psalm comes to a prayerful petition to God for help and salvation: 'O Lord, save (*YHWH hôšî'â nā'*)! O Lord, deliver!' (LXX). Expressions very similar to *YHWH hôšî'â* occur a number of times in the Psalms, expressing a request for God's help:

> Help, Lord (*hôšî'â YHWH*), for the godly man ceases! For the faithful disappear from among the sons of men (Ps. 12:1).

> Save, Lord (*YHWH hôšî'â*)! May the King answer us when we call' (Ps. 20:9).

> Save (*hôšî'â*) Your people, and bless Your inheritance; shepherd them also, and bear them up forever (Ps. 28:9).

> That Your beloved may be delivered, save (*hôšî'â*) with Your right hand, and hear me (Ps. 60:5, repeated in Ps. 108:6).

The Greek word Hosanna corresponds to a Hebrew word composed of two parts: *hôšî'â*, meaning 'save', 'deliver' or 'help'; and *nā'*, an enclitic particle indicating the depth of the petitioner's need. The use of the original Hebrew expression—in the mouths of those who welcomed Christ into Jerusalem—can be translated: 'Save us now, O Lord.' To understand the origin of this call, we must turn to the rites carried out on certain ancient Jewish feast days, in which this exclamation was used.

Psalms 113–118 formed a set known as the 'Hallel Psalms' because they were chanted on the Feast of Tabernacles and the Passover, and the people were to chant Halleluiah after certain verses and at the end of every psalm. The Hallel Psalms were chanted in a rhythmic, monotonous tone, sentence by sentence, as one might hear in Jewish synagogues today, as well as during the Psalmody in the Christian churches.

During the seven days dedicated to the Feast of Tabernacles, the priests would take up tree branches in their hands and go out in a splendid procession, circling the altar of burnt offerings crying out: 'Lord, save us (*hôšî'â nā*)! Save us (*hôšî'â nā*)!' On the seventh day of the feast, this procession was carried out seven times. The repeated cry of the people expressed their petition to God to cause the rains to fall. The set of prayers recited during the procession of the Feast of Tabernacles came to be known as the *hôša'nôt*, and the seventh day of the feast as *Hôša'nā' Rabbâ* 'The Great Hosannah'.[62]

The practice of waving tree branches and palm leaves has its source in a particular interpretation of the verse: 'Let the field be joyful, and all that is in it. Let all the trees of the woods rejoice' (Ps. 96:12). One of the ancient rabbis connected the joyful motion of the trees with the joy of the people at having obtained justification before God the just judge. It was believed that

---

[62] Cf. Eduard Lohse, 'ὡσαννά,' in *TDNT*, IX: 682.

when God came down to save His people, bringing them forgiveness and redemption, the whole creation would share in the celebration, rejoicing in this salvation. So also, the rain which the people implored God to send down would bless the people of Israel, and with them, the whole creation.

In the period between the Old and New Testaments —known as the Intertestamental Period—the Feast of Tabernacles became associated with feast of dedication (or *Hanukkah*), celebrated in the Spring Month, in commemoration of Judas Maccabaeus' victorious revolution against Antiochus IV. In 163 BC, Judas Maccabaeus led the Jews in rebellion against the Seleucid ruler Antiochus IV who had offered a pig in sacrifice to idols in the Jerusalem Temple, prompting the Jews to revolt against him and stage a revolution. The revolution succeeded, allowing them to cleanse the Temple and celebrate the Feast of Tabernacles. This revolution granted the Jewish people a period of political and religious freedom, and its yearly commemoration became known as Hanukkah or the Feast of Dedication.

The word *Hosanna!* (*hôšî'â nā'*) became a prominent cry at these yearly celebrations of the Dedication in which the people commemorated the salvation God had granted them. A desire grew among the people for God to send them a saviour like Judas Maccabaeus who could bring them freedom and purify their worship from the impurities that had accrued to it.

ANBA EPIPHANIUS

In the days of the Lord Jesus though, the word *Hosanna* had acquired a strong association with the idea of the coming of the Messiah, who would grant political freedom to the nation and reestablish the religious freedom the people had obtained at the hands of Judas Maccabaeus.

It is worth noting that the people's cries of Hosanna! to the Lord Jesus as He entered Jerusalem directly preceded His purification of the Temple and the driving out of the dove sellers and moneychangers. When the people cried out, chanting with the words of Psalm 118:25, 'Hosanna to the Son of David! Blessed is He who comes in the name of the Lord! Hosanna in the highest!' (Matt. 21:9), the Lord Jesus entered the Temple and purified it, restoring the respect and dignity due to it as a place for the worship of God. It was well known among the general populace and among the clergy that Psalm 118 constituted a direct prophecy about the coming of the Messiah. The people's cry was a Messianic echo and an expression of their eagerness for the appearance of the Christ — a new Joshua — who would bring about the salvation of their nation and purify their worship and their political lives along with their hearts from all the impurities and contradictions that afflicted them.

Of course, the people did not know that the One entering Jerusalem before their eyes was the very Messiah whose coming they had awaited for so long, and who they expected would fulfil all their hopes and expectations. Christ's character was not obviously Messianic to the minds of the people, or even in the minds of most of the disciples, to the extent that one of them sold Him, another denied Him, and the entire people cried 'Crucify Him! Crucify Him!'

Hosanna in the Gospel of St Matthew

If we turn to the people's cries as recorded in the Gospel of Matthew, we find the phrase 'to the Son of David' added directly after the word 'Hosannna' — 'Hosanna to the Son of David' — which brings in a level of ambiguity. If 'Hosanna' means 'Save now!', what is the meaning of 'Save now, to the Son of David'? It is very likely that the people repeated this cry in the Hebrew language as a sort of patriotic zeal, since Hebrew was their native language and the language of worship in the Temple. In this instance, the people used the Hebrew preposition l^e- before 'Son of David' adding the meaning 'unto' or 'for'. Linguists have established that this letter could also be used as a vocative particle (English 'O'), so the cry could be translated 'Hosanna (i.e. save us) O Son of David!' This would imply that the people were accepting Jesus as a political messiah and leader come to save them from the Roman rule.[63]

Yet the Greek text still stands in need of interpretation. The Greek expression 'to the son of David (*tō yiō Dauíd*) cannot be translated as 'O Son of David'. Why

---

[63] Cf. Marvin H. Pope, 'Hosanna: What it Really Means', *Bible Review* 4,2 (1988): 16–25; *Id.*, "Vestiges of Vocative Lamedh in the Bible", in *Ugarit-Forschungen* 20 (1988): 201-207.

then did St Matthew insist on translating the Hebrew phrase into this Greek form? It is clear that St Matthew was indicating the salvation brought about by Christ on the Cross. The connection of this ancient cry of 'Hosanna!' to the victory of Judas Maccabaeus, the celebration of the Feast of Dedication, and the verse 'Blessed is He who comes in the name of the Lord' (Ps. 118:26) had given the phrase 'Hosanna' a new meaning which St Matthew wanted to emphasise. This meaning is clearest after the Lord Jesus' Crucifixion, Death and Resurrection from the dead, for the word *Hosanna* became chiefly an expression of joy at the salvation brought about by the Lord Jesus, rather than a plea for help. Here, St Matthew's meaning is 'Glory to the one who has given us salvation, glory to the Son of David!'[64]

For St Matthew then, the word *Hosanna* implies that all the Messianic hopes and expectations have been realised in Jesus. A Greek reader of Matthew's Gospel would clearly understand the significance of the word *Hosanna* without needing to refer back to its historical meaning in Hebrew, because he would share St Matthew's joy at the salvation effected by the Lord Jesus; since he is reading the Gospel after the Lord's Resurrection from the dead, he has accepted Christ as a redeemer and saviour from sin, not as a political saviour or leader.

---

[64] TN: This is the meaning assumed by some modern English translations such as the *Contemporary English Version* which has: 'Hooray for the Son of David'.

HOSANNA TO THE SON OF DAVID

Of course, the people who received the Lord Jesus would not have understood their own cries as in this doxological sense. Nonetheless, just as He did with many expressions in the Old Testament, the Lord Jesus brought out the true meaning behind the people's cries. Even though most of the people who had seen Jesus, heard His teaching and witnessed His miracles did not understand the true meaning of His coming, the Lord Jesus fulfilled and answered the people's need for salvation in the way that He Himself willed; a way which the people did not understand until after the Lord's Resurrection from the dead. After the descent of the Holy Spirit, the people began to become increasingly aware of the salvation which the Lord Jesus had achieved for them—it was a salvation from sin, a liberation from the dominion of Satan and power granted them from the Lord to live in the freedom proper to sons and daughters, as children of God and members of His household.

'Hosanna' in the Liturgy and Tradition of the Church

The word *Hosanna* entered the Church's prayers at a very early stage.[65] It was the doxological sense of the word that entered the Christian Church, not the petitionary sense. It is mentioned in the *Didache*—a work which records for us the liturgical prayers practiced in the early Church—that when the prayers of the Lord's

---

[65] Cf. Eduard Lohse, 'ὡσαννά,' in *TDNT*, IX: 684.

Supper is to be celebrated, the following prayer is to be recited:

> Let grace come and let this world pass away. Hosanna to the God of David. If any man be holy, let him come! if any man be not, let him repent: Maranathà, Amen.[66]

This prayer is clearly not taken from the Gospel, but rather from the liturgical tradition practiced by the disciples, and which they taught the earliest churches.

The word also found its way into the congregational responses of the Liturgy of St Gregory:

> Holy, Holy, Holy, Lord of Sabaoth, heaven and earth are full of Your holy glory. Hosanna in the highest, blessed is He who has come and comes in the name of the Lord. Hosanna in the highest.[67]

The word *Hosanna* also acquired an eschatological significance in the Church, and became directly connected with the phrase *Maranathà*, an expression of the imminence of the Lord's coming. In addition to the passage from the *Didache* cited above which includes both expressions together, Eusebius of Caesarea's *Ecclesiastical History* contains an account of the martyrdom of St James the Righteous, brother of the Lord, which demonstrates this link between the word *Hosanna* and the imminence of the Lord's coming. When the Jews

---

[66] *Didache* 10.6. Cf. Kirsopp Lake (ed.), *The Apostolic Fathers*, Loeb Classical Library (Harvard University Press, 1912): 325.

[67] *Kitāb al-Ḥūlāǧī al-Muqaddas* (Wādī al-Naṭrūn: Dayr al-Suryān Press, 2016: 571-572).

HOSANNA TO THE SON OF DAVID

had set the Apostle James on the side of the Temple, just before his martyrdom:

> He answered with a loud voice, 'Why do you ask me concerning Jesus, the Son of Man? He himself sits in heaven at the right hand of the great Power, and is about to come upon the clouds of heaven.' And when many were fully convinced and gloried in the testimony of James, and said, 'Hosanna to the Son of David,' these same scribes and pharisees said again to one another, 'We have done badly in supplying such testimony to Jesus'.[68]

It seems that the original Hebrew meaning of the cry *Hosanna* was lost with the passage of time, especially in Greek-speaking churches. In his book *The Instructor* or *Pedagogue*, St Clement of Alexandria explains the meaning of *Hosanna* 'as light, and glory, and praise, with supplication to the Lord: this is the meaning of the expression Hosanna.'[69] Just as in the early Church, it is possible to use the word *Hosanna* in worship today with both its meanings: as a plea for help from God, and as a glorification of the God who has become salvation for us. Christ has effected salvation for us through His atoning Death on the Cross and His Resurrection from the dead. He now sits at the right hand of the Father, interceding for those who believe in Him, offering the guarantee of our justification before God for 'Who shall bring a charge against God's elect? It is God who justifies. Who

---

[68] Eusebius of Caesarea, *Ecclesiastical History*, II.23.13–14 (*NPNF* 1/1:126).

[69] Clement of Alexandria, *Instructor* 1.5 (*ANF* 2:212).

is he who condemns? It is Christ who died, and furthermore is also risen, who is even at the right hand of God, who also makes intercession for us' (Rom. 8:33–4)

Humanity manifestly rejoices in the faith that Christ Himself intercedes for us before God, as though He were saying to the Father, '*Hosanna* (Save, now!), for the sake of My children, those who believe in My name.' We can also say that the Holy Spirit offers a *Hosanna*-type intercession to the Father for our sake, for 'the Spirit Himself makes intercession for us with groanings which cannot be uttered' (Rom. 8:26). The cry of *Hosanna* with which the people greeted Christ at His entry into Jerusalem was a plea for help (though at that time, they were asking for help on the bodily and political level). But now, it has become the cry of the Church for God to complete our salvation, and an expression of praise and thanksgiving to the One who through His Death on our behalf became our salvation: 'To You is the power, and the glory, and the blessing and the honour forever. Amen. My Lord Jesus Christ, my Good Saviour. My strength and my praise is the Lord who became my holy salvation.'[70]

---

[70] Doxology of the Eve and of the Day of Great Friday of the Holy Pascha, according to the Coptic Orthodox rite.

GIVE TO CAESAR WHAT IS CAESAR'S AND TO GOD WHAT IS GOD'S

On the Sunday known as Palm Sunday, the Lord Jesus went into Jerusalem, drove the merchants from the Temple and overturned the tables of the moneychangers and the seats of the dove vendors. His conduct angered the scribes and Pharisees and elders of the people, so they approached Him saying: 'By what authority are You doing these things? And who gave You this authority?' (Matt. 21:23). Jesus answered their question with another question about the baptism of John, whether it was from heaven or from men. When they refused to answer, He began to rebuke them with various parables such as the parable of the two sons (cf. Matt. 21:27–32), the parable of the vinedressers who killed those sent to them before finally killing the son and heir (cf. Matt. 21:33–44), and the parable of the wedding of the king's son (cf. Matt. 22:1–13).

The Pharisees withdrew from the scene and began to plot among themselves how they might catch Him in His words. They sent spies to Him 'who pretended to be righteous, that they might seize on His words, in order to deliver Him to the power and the authority of the governor' (Luke 20:20). They launched into a long introduction filled with words of praise before posing their question: 'Teacher, we know that You are true, and care about no one; for You do not regard the person of men, but teach the way of God in truth. Is it lawful to pay taxes to Caesar, or not? Shall we pay, or shall we not pay?' (Mark 12:14).

Clearly, this was a straightforward question that required a straightforward answer. Why then, all this flattering introduction? Why, unless the question concealed a dangerous trap within its folds? The spies who brought this question belonged to two opposing factions. The first were disciples of the Pharisees, a sect of theologians who kept the teachings of the Law and its statutes, and who confessed no rule except God's, rejecting all foreign rule. Naturally, these men rejected the idea of paying taxes to Caesar.

The second sect were the Herodians, partisans of Herod's house who—despite their loyalty to the ruling family—discouraged the payment of taxes to Caesar. There was at least one man among Christ's own disciples who belonged to the party of the Zealots, i.e. Simon the Zealot. The Zealots were one of the most fanatical Jewish factions hostile to the Roman occupation who vigorously opposed the payment of any taxes to Rome. The Lord Jesus Himself was from Galilee, the Judean province which had staged an armed revolt against the Roman occupation.

All these circumstances conspired to make this question a severe trial. To respond either way—either in favour of paying taxes or against it—would bring countless perils. If the Lord Jesus responded by rejecting the payment of taxes, He would be giving the spies what they were hoping for, grounds to hand Him over to the ruling authorities on the charge of inciting a revolt against Rome, a crime punishable by death. But if He responded in favour of paying taxes, He would lose the sympathies of all the people around Him, and place Himself in direct confrontation with the scribes and Pharisees and elders of the people, along with some of His own disciples. In this way, the Pharisees posed their question, and awaited the response.[71]

The Lord Jesus was not deceived by their words of praise and flattery, for He looks not at the outward appearance but at the heart (cf. 1 Sam. 16:7). 'But Jesus perceived their wickedness, and said, "Why do you test Me, you hypocrites? Show Me the tax money"' (Matt. 22:18–19). So they brought Him a denarius, the currency in which the tax was paid, which bore an image of Tiberius Caesar, along with his name and title. He asked them:

> "Whose image and inscription is this?" They said to Him, "Caesar's." And He said to them, "Render therefore to Caesar the things that are Caesar's, and to God the things that are God's." When they had heard these words, they marvelled, and left Him and went their way (Matt. 22:20–2).

The Pharisees were not expecting this answer at all; they had assumed He would side with them against the

---

[71] Cf. J. W. Shepard, *The Christ of the Gospels* (Grand Rapids, MI: Eerdmans, 1971): 497–8.

payment of taxes. The reason for the Pharisees' shock and the reason they retreated without a word was that they had understood the meaning of Lord's response. His response was not simply that they should pay Roman taxes with the currency bearing Caesar's image and then offer God His due from the Temple currency (the Jewish *šeqel*) which does not bear Caesar's image. This was far from the Lord's intended meaning. Otherwise, one of them would have reasonably objected, saying, "Everything we own belongs to God; even Caesar himself is God's possession! How then should we give from what is not ours to one who is not worthy of it?"

The Lord Jesus therefore seized this opportunity to set aright a widespread error rife throughout every part of the Roman Empire. Christianity was born into a world in which the cult of Caesar was widespread; Caesar was widely held to be a god. The Empire had very extensive borders, and was comprised of peoples with their own distinct languages, religions and customs. What held this vast empire together was not simply the Roman army which was dispersed throughout the nations. The one shared religious cult which was imposed upon them all—the cult of Caesar—was another, perhaps even greater a cause of unity.

Political and military cohesion was important, but religious cohesion was more important still. The Roman state was well aware of this, and strove to spread the cult of Caesar. Rome never opposed the native religions of the peoples who came under their banner, so long as those peoples consented to adopt the worship of Caesar alongside their existing beliefs. However, they had little patience for any people who refused to submit to their beliefs; they interacted with such peoples very particularly, and expected them to rebel at any moment.

The worship of Caesar, as a historical reality, sheds light on many verses in the New Testament, including the verse: 'Render therefore to Caesar the things that are Caesar's, and to God the things that are God's' (Matt 22:21). It reveals the parallel between Christianity and the cult of the emperor; between the place of the Lord Jesus in the Christian religion and the place of the emperor in the state religion, and the titles each of them bore.

THE TITLE OF KÝRIOS (LORD)

The Greek word *kýrios* means *lord* or *master*, and was one of the titles applied to the emperor. Likewise, it was an official title of the Lord Jesus, because it was the word used in the Septuagint version of the Old Testament to translate the sacred Hebrew name *YHWH*. As a title, therefore, it is not simply a term of honour, but indicates divinity, especially when it was used to refer to God, or as it was later used to refer to the emperor.

This fact helps us understand those verses in which the Apostle Paul uses this term in his first letter to the Corinthians:

> For even if there are so-called gods, whether in heaven or on earth (as there are many gods and many lords), yet for us there is one God, the Father, of whom are all things,

and we for Him (1 Cor. 8:5–6).

St Paul makes this statement as part of his discourse on the importance of believers keeping themselves separate from the cults of pagan Greece. The Corinthian faithful were obliged to reject any kind of worship offered to the emperor, and to avoid partaking in any rituals performed for the pagan gods of Greece. For even if Greece had filled the heavens with the names of many gods, and the Romans had filled the earth with the worship of their king, we know none in heaven but one God—the Father—the source of all creation, and we do not belong but to Him. And we know no other Lord but Jesus Christ, His only Son, by whom all things were made, and one with the Father.[72]

The Lord Jesus refers to the practice of venerating Caesar beyond the norm when He said, 'The kings of the Gentiles exercise lordship [*kyrieúousin*] over them' (Luke 22:25). The phrase *exercise lordship* does not simply mean that the kings of the Gentiles (Caesar and other like him) exercise authority over the people with the power of their office, but that they conduct themselves as *lords* (*kýrioi*). This same word is applied to Jesus: 'For to this end Christ died and lived again, that he might be Lord [*kyrieúsē*] both of the dead and of the living' (Rom. 14:9). St Paul makes this clear when he calls Christ: '… the blessed and only Sovereign, the King of kings (literally, *king of those who rule as kings*) and Lord

---

[72] Cf. Werner Foerster, 'Κύριος', *TDNT*, III: 1091.

of lords (literally, *Lord of those who exercise lordship*)' (1 Tim. 6:15).[73]

Christianity's refusal to call human beings Lord and their reservation of this title for the Lord Jesus was not simply a result of the political circumstances; nor was it a new teaching intended to oppose a widespread error. Rather, it goes back to the dawn of Christianity, when the angel announced the birth of the Child Jesus to the shepherds, for he spoke to them saying, 'For there is born to you this day in the city of David a Saviour, who is Christ *the Lord*' (Luke 2:11). As if to say, 'Even if there are some on earth who call themselves 'lords', behold, I announce to you the birth of the true and only Lord.'

After the Lord Jesus' Resurrection from the dead, the disciples' chief confession, which came on the tongue of the apostle Thomas, was to address the Lord Jesus as 'my Lord and my God' (John 20:27). For this reason, when St John saw the Lord Jesus on the shore of the Sea of Tiberias after His Resurrection, he said to Peter, 'It is *the Lord*' (John 21:7).

The confusion between what belongs to Caesar and what belongs to God clearly appears in the trial of the Apostle Paul, for Festus the governor declares, 'I have nothing certain to write to my lord [*kyríō*] concerning him' (Acts 25:26). Here, Festus describes the Emperor

---

[73] TN: The literal translations in brackets were added by Anba Epiphanius. In Greek, these phrases are *basileús tōn basileuóntōn* and *kýrios tōn kyrieuóntōn*.

Nero as his lord and master, for he refers as 'Lord', that is, a god, one to whom worship is due.

This very title is the one which the holy martyr Polycarp (died 156 AD) rejected when he was brought to trial. The ruler Herod asked him, 'For what harm is there in saying, "Lord Caesar", and sacrificing and saving your life?'[74] Because he refused to confuse what is due to Caesar with what is due to God, St Polycarp received the crown of martyrdom.

Accordingly, St Paul sums up the Christian position that the title 'Lord' should, in its proper sense, only be applied to the Lord Jesus and none besides Him:

> Therefore God also has highly exalted Him and given Him the name which is above every name, that at the name of Jesus every knee should bow, of those in heaven, and of those on earth, and of those under the earth, and that every tongue should confess that *Jesus Christ is Lord*, to the glory of God the Father (Phil. 2:9–11).

THE TITLE OF THEÓS (GOD)

The title *Lord* was not the only title popularly applied to the emperor; the people also referred to him with the title of *theós*, that is 'god.' It was said of Augustus Caesar that he was 'god of god' and that he was 'the god Caesar'. The Emperor was generally called 'our god and our master.'[75] The people even flattered King Herod with

---

[74] Eusebius of Caesarea, *Ecclesiastical History* IV.15.15 (*NPNF* 1/1:190).

[75] Cf. Ethelbert Stauffer, 'Θεός', *TDNT*, III: 69.

this title, though he was the king of the Jews: 'So on a set day Herod, arrayed in royal apparel, sat on his throne and gave an oration to them. And the people kept shouting, "The voice of a god and not of a man!"' (Acts 12:21–22). Here, we manifestly see what belongs to God being usurped and ascribed to man. Accordingly, heaven's intervention was swift: 'Then immediately an angel of the Lord struck him, because he did not give glory to God. And he was eaten by worms and died' (Acts 12:23).

The Title of Sōtḗr (Saviour)

The kings of old were also honoured with the title of *sōtḗr,* 'saviour,' implying that it is the king who saves the people from the woes of war, famine and hardship. Emperors bore this title as a mark of divinity, not merely as a political title.[76] Of the emperors of Rome, at least eight bore the title 'saviour of the world'.[77] Because Heaven sought to set right this error and restore to God what is due to Him, the archangel Gabriel declared that He who was to be born in Bethlehem would be called Jesus, 'for *He will save His people* from their sins' (Matt. 1:21). The angel also announced to the shepherds, '[T]here is born to you this day in the city of David *a Saviour*, who is Christ the Lord' (Luke 2:11).

---

[76] Cf. *GELNT*: 808.

[77] TN: Beginning with Julius Caesar himself, virtually every emperor of the early Christian era who held the throne for any length of time bore the title *sōtḗr tēs oikouménēs*, 'saviour of the world', or some variation on it. See Craig R Koester, '"Saviour of the World": John 4:42', *Journal of Biblical Literature* 109, vol. 4 (1990): 665–680.

ANBA EPIPHANIUS

When the Lord Jesus began His ministry, and the people witnessed His wonders and miracles, they believed that He was the saviour who had come to save them from their sins, and they confessed Him saying, 'This is indeed the Christ, the Saviour of the world' (John 4:42).

Therefore, give to Caesar what is Caesar's, and to God what is God's. Give to Caesar your taxes paid with this world's money, for he is a king to you and money, along with everything it can buy, are earthly things destined to pass away. 'Render therefore to all their due: taxes to whom taxes are due, customs to whom customs, fear to whom fear, honour to whom honour' (Rom. 13:7). But as for God, give Him your hearts, your souls and your spirits, for these are not your possessions, 'for you were bought at a price; therefore glorify God in your body and in your spirit, which are God's' (1 Cor. 6:20).

Give to Caesar respect, honour, submission and obedience: 'Let every soul be subject to the governing authorities. For there is no authority except from God' (Rom 13:1). But as for God, give Him worship and adoration: 'You shall worship the Lord your God, and Him only you shall serve' (Matt. 4:10).

Give to Caesar the denarius which bears his image, but to God, give yourself, for you bear the image of His Son (cf. Rom. 8:29).

THE BRONZE SERPENT

In the Lord Jesus' conversation with Nicodemus, a member of the Sanhedrin, about the second birth, Nicodemus asked Him how this birth was possible; that is, how can a man go back into his mother's womb when he is old and be born? In response, the Lord Jesus explained that the second birth was not a fleshly birth, for 'that which is born of the flesh is flesh, and that which is born of the Spirit is spirit' (John 3:6). The Lord then commented about this conversation saying, "And as Moses lifted up the serpent in the wilderness, even so must the Son of Man be lifted up" (John 3:14). What was the serpent that Moses lifted up, and did the Lord Jesus use it as a symbol of His being lifted up on the Cross?

The Bronze Serpent of Moses

When the children of Israel were sojourning from Mount Hor along the Red Sea in order to skirt around the land of Edom, while they were on their way to the land which God had promised them, they fell into their old habit of murmuring against God and His prophet Moses:

> And the people spoke against God and against Moses: "Why have you brought us up out of Egypt to die in the wilderness? For there is no food and no water, and our soul loathes this worthless bread [i.e. the manna] (Num. 21:5).

ANBA EPIPHANIUS

The people had forgotten the wonders God had wrought before them by the hands of Moses the Prophet, His delivering them from Pharaoh and the Egyptians, the parting of the Red Sea beneath their feet, the coming of manna from Heaven for them, the comfort brought to them by the wind, and the water gushing out from the solid rock. The people had forgotten all of these wonders in a moment of distress and murmured against God and the blessings He had bestowed on them. God's chastisement upon them was severe:

> So the Lord sent fiery serpents [*hann^{e}ḥāšîm haśś^{e}rāfîm*] among the people, and they bit the people; and many of the people of Israel died (Num. 21:6).

The phrase "fiery serpents" refers to a breed of vipers common in the Sinai Desert, identifiable by the bright red spots and wavy lines on its skin; the Bedouins greatly feared it on account of its deadly venom.

The word "fiery" used to describe the serpents is the same word used by Isaiah the Prophet to describe one of the heavenly orders he saw in his vision. The word used was *seraphim*:

> Above it stood seraphim [*ś^{e}rāfîm*]; each one had six wings… Then one of the seraphim flew to me, having in his hand a live coal which he had taken with the tongs from the altar. And he touched my mouth with it (Isa. 6:2,6).

The word *seraphim* describes the bright and luminous appearance of these heavenly beings which stand around the throne of God. Therefore, the word *fiery*, when

THE BRONZE SERPENT

applied to the serpents, referred to the colour of their bright red spots more than to their deadly venom.

When the deadly serpents attacked the people, and those slain began to fall left and right, the people cried out and declared their repentance so that God might lift away the deadly evil:

> Therefore the people came to Moses, and said, "We have sinned, for we have spoken against the Lord and against you; pray to the Lord that He take away the serpents from us." So Moses prayed for the people. Then the Lord said to Moses, "Make a fiery serpent, and set it on a pole; and it shall be that everyone who is bitten, when he looks at it, shall live." So Moses made a bronze serpent, and put it on a pole; and so it was, if a serpent had bitten anyone, when he looked at the bronze serpent, he lived (Num. 21:7–9).

In interpreting the statue of the serpent on the pole, some commentators have connected it to various notions in ancient paganism associated with both serpents and healing. For instance, there was an ancient belief among the pagan peoples that anything with the power to bring disease also had the power to provide healing, that is, it contained both the disease and the cure. This belief is still widespread in some quarters today.

The snake's ability to shed its old skin and reveal new skin formed beneath it, indicated to some a power to create new life.[78]

---

[78] Cf. Isaac Hunt, "Serpent (as symbol)" in *New Catholic Encyclopedia*, XIII (New York, NY: Thomson Gale 2003): 21.

There was another ancient belief that some parts of a viper's body had the power to bring healing, which is the reason ancient physicians used the bodies of serpents in the concoction of some medicines.

One of the greatest examples of this association between serpents and healing power is the symbolic rod carried by Asclepius, the Greek god of medicine, which is a serpent coiled around a staff. Over time, this symbol became conflated with the rod borne by the Greek god Hermes, a staff adorned with two serpents, known as the *Caduceus*, which was a symbol of peace rather than healing. As a result of this conflation, the double-snaked Staff of Hermes became a symbol of physicians (for instance, in the logo of the American Medical Association).

But none of these pagan ideas or symbols can be applied in any way to the bronze serpent made by the prophet Moses. The myths associated with the Greek god of medicine are totally removed from the history of Israel, because they are myths which only arose many generations after the exodus of the children of Israel.

Nor should we look for any pagan practices which prescribe the lifting up of a bronze serpent, especially in the days of Moses, for God's command to the people at that time was very clear. The second of the Ten Commandments forbade the raising up of any likeness or image of any creature: 'You shall not make for yourself a carved image—any likeness of anything that is in heaven above, or that is in the earth beneath, or that is in the

THE BRONZE SERPENT

water under the earth' (Ex. 20:4). Likewise, God had commanded the people not to imitate the neighbouring pagan nations, and not to follow any of their customs or traditions: 'According to the doings of the land of Egypt, where you dwelt, you shall not do; and according to the doings of the land of Canaan, where I am bringing you, you shall not do; nor shall you walk in their ordinances' (Lev. 18:3).

In addition, the bronze serpent was not the fruit of Moses' own thoughts but a direct commandment from God (cf. Num. 21:8). Therefore, we must search for the meaning of the bronze serpent in the Holy Bible, not in pagan mythology.

Since God had already warned the people against turning to sorcery or amulets or any such things, His intention was certainly not to make the people believe that the bronze serpent had any power in and of itself to cure the vipers' deadly poison. The mere act of looking toward the bronze serpent suspended on the pole has no significance apart from God's direction that they should do so. What matters here is faith in God's words, not the serpent itself. Trust in God was all the people needed. Faith was the only remedy for their sufferings, their rebellion, and insubordination, and likewise, it was only faith that allowed God to enter their lives and grant them healing.

The obedience of the people in going out and looking to the serpent lifted on the pole resembles the obedience of the man born blind, whom the Lord Jesus

ANBA EPIPHANIUS

commanded to go and wash in the pool of Siloam. The water of the pool of Siloam had no power to grant sight to the blind; rather, what granted him sight was his faithfulness to the Lord Jesus' command (cf. John 9:6, 7). In both cases, going out to look at the serpent and going to wash in the pool Siloam confirmed their faith in God's commandment, and it was this faith which allowed God to grant them healing.

King Hezekiah Breaks the Bronze Serpent

At the time of Hezekiah, king of Judah, the people fell prey to many pagan customs. One such custom was the veneration of religious artefacts. The bronze serpent was still among them, and the people began to offer incense to it. In this way, the bronze serpent became an idol, and the people began to worship it. At those times when the people did not feel the presence of God among them, they sought for any alternative symbols, however holy they might be, and approached them with worship and veneration, forgetting that God is spirit and that worship directed to Him ought to be in spirit and truth (John 4:24). The purpose of the bronze serpent was in this way entirely subverted; instead of being a sign pointing to life and healing, it became a cause of sin and death.

King Hezekiah, being a righteous ruler, was compelled to take harsh measures to put a stop to this idolatrous worship:

> He removed the high places and broke the sacred pillars, cut down the wooden image and broke in pieces the

THE BRONZE SERPENT

bronze serpent that Moses had made; for until those days the children of Israel burned incense to it, and called it Nehushtan [*nᵉḥōštān,* derived from *nᵉḥōšet*] (2 Kings 4:18).

THE BRONZE SERPENT AS A TYPE OF CHRIST ON THE CROSS

When Nicodemus asked the Lord Jesus about how the second birth could take place, the Lord answered by providing an image. He said that for a man to be born a second time, that is, from above, it is necessary that the Son of Man should first be lifted up as Moses lifted up the serpent in the wilderness (John 3:14). John's Gospel makes clear that the lifting up of the Son of Man is His Death on the Cross: '"And I, if I am lifted up from the earth, will draw all peoples to Myself." This He said, signifying by what Death He would die' (John 12:32–33). It is clear from the expression the Lord uses with Nicodemus about the lifting up of the Son of Man is a confirmation of the necessity of the Cross. Perhaps Nicodemus also understood 'lifting up from the earth' as a reference to the Cross. At that time, apart from crucifixion, there was no other means by which a man could die suspended above the earth like the bronze serpent.

For some commentators, this lifting up from the earth refers not simply to being lifted up on the Cross, but rather to three events of which the Cross was the first, then the Resurrection, and then the Ascension. The Cross cannot be separated from the Resurrection and

Ascension, even if the verse does not include any explicit reference to them.[79]

The Lord affirmed in His conversation with Nicodemus that it was necessary for Him to be lifted up, but He did not shed any light on why this was necessary. However, He revealed later that it was fitting for Him to be crucified, because apart from the Cross, no man would be saved. The Lord Jesus said that as a result of His being lifted up, everyone who believed in Him would have eternal life (cf. John 3:14–15).

After Moses lifted the Bronze Serpent on the pole, everyone who was bitten by the fiery serpents and struck by their deadly poison was compelled to heed the Lord's command and believe in His words. They had to go out and look upon the hanging serpent and be healed. In this same way, when the Lord Jesus was lifted on the Cross, all those who looked upon Him in faith lived.

The same Lord who long ago declared His love for the children of Israel—'When Israel was a child, I loved him' (Hos. 11:1)—and ordered the Bronze Serpent to be made for them, this same Lord revealed to Nicodemus His love for us: 'For God so loved the world that He gave His only begotten Son, that whoever believes in

---

[79] Cf. Raymond E. Brown, *The Gospel According to John*, The Anchor Bible Series, edited by W. F. Albright & D. N. Freedman, Vol. 29 (Doubleday, 1966): 145–46.

THE BRONZE SERPENT

Him should not perish but have everlasting life' (John 3:16).

It is worth noting here that when the Lord Jesus reminded Nicodemus of the Bronze Serpent which Moses lifted in the wilderness so that those stung by the fiery serpents would be healed in looking at it, He wanted to show him that this was a type of His own lifting up on the Cross and His Death for our sake, as an atonement for our sins which He bore in His holy body. For in ancient times, the serpent represented sin and evil, and the Lord Jesus—even though He committed no sin, nor was any deceit found in this mouth (cf. Isa. 53:9) —nonetheless He came in the likeness of sinful flesh (cf. Rom. 8:3) and bore our sins in His body upon the tree, (1 Pet. 2:23). He became sin for our sake as St Paul said (2 Cor. 5:21). What the Lord Jesus was referring to, then, was that the hanging of the serpent upon the pole was a sign of His being lifted on the Cross bearing our sins. On this point, St Cyril the Great writes:

> The serpents were leaping on those of Israel in the desert. And as they were falling like ears of corn, immeasurably distressed at the danger that visited them unexpectedly, they uttered the most pitiful cries and kept calling for salvation from above and from God. Since as God he is good and compassionate, he commands Moses to raise up a bronze serpent for them, and by this command in particular he orders them to rehearse beforehand salvation by faith. For the medicine to those bitten was to look at the face of the serpent put before them, and faith along with what was seen worked deliverance at the last extremity for

those who saw it ... And so God the Word came 'in the likeness of sinful flesh in order to condemn sin in the flesh' (Rom 8:3), as it is written. He came to be made the procurer of indestructible salvation for those who gaze at him by a more intent faith or by searching the divine dogmas. The fact that the serpent was set up on a high base certainly indicates the fact that Christ became known and distinguished so that he was unknown to no one; or it indicates that he was lifted from the earth, as he himself says somewhere (Jn 12:32), by his suffering on the Cross.[80]

Thus, Christ on the Cross 'wiped out the handwriting of requirements that was against us, which was contrary to us. And He has taken it out of the way, having nailed it to the Cross. Having disarmed principalities and powers, He made a public spectacle of them, triumphing over them in it,' that is, in the Cross (Col. 2:14–15).

Let those who have been stung by sin and have its deadly poison spread throughout their body lift their eyes to the One who died once for their sake, Who is now alive and the Life-giver. They shall feel the tremors of a new life running through their inward parts, renewing their thoughts, their affections, their hopes and their desires. The Lord Jesus revealed in His conversation with Nicodemus the mystery of new life which He granted to him and to all who believe in Him; all that

---

[80] Cyril of Alexandria, *Commentary on John*, II:2, 1, trans. David R. Maxwell, ed. Joel C. Elowsky (IVP Academic: Downers Grove, IL, 2013): 100–1.

remains for us now is to look upon the Lord Jesus in faith, that we might inherit eternal life.

THE LORD JESUS
WAS CRUCIFIED FOR MY SAKE

In the doxology of Passion Week which we repeat many times each day, we say in the first verse:

> To You is the power and the glory and the blessing and the honour forever, Amen. Emmanuel *our* God and *our* king.

The plural *our* is used. In the second verse, we say:

> *My* Lord Jesus Christ, *my* good savior

The text here is in the singular. The intention here is to affirm that what Christ accomplished on the Cross cannot be received without personal faith. Likewise, it affirms that Christ, when He died on the Cross, died for *my* sake and for *your* sake, personally; He died for the sake of each and every one of us, by name. We find the Apostle Paul confirming this idea when he says, '[He] loved me (*me, personally*) and gave Himself for me' (Gal. 2:20).

The Creed which the Church recites every day contains this phrase: 'Who for our sake, and for our salvation, came down from heaven and was incarnate of the Holy Spirit and the Virgin Mary, became man, and was crucified for us'. This important theological expression indicates that Christ's Crucifixion was for my sake and for your sake; His love for us is a love both personal and very deep. We could recite Isaiah's hymn of the Suffering Servant in the plural as well as in the singular:

> Surely He has borne *my* griefs and carried *my* sorrows… He was wounded for *my* transgressions, He was bruised for *my* iniquities; the chastisement for *my* peace was upon Him, and by His stripes *I am* healed (Isa. 53:4–6).

For my sake and on account of my sins, He was hung upon the Cross in order to grant me forgiveness.

In his *Abridgement of the Life of Jesus Christ*, the French natural philosopher and mathematician Blaise Pascal (1623–1662)—one of the greatest thinkers humanity has ever produced—recounts how he came to faith. He writes, 'In the middle of the night, 23 November 1654, the Lord Jesus spoke to me saying, "Blaise, I was thinking of you throughout my passion."' This experience was the cause of the faith of this philosopher. He felt that the Cross of Christ was for his sake, personally. Christ said, 'Blaise, it was for your sake that I bore all of this.' The Lord Jesus suffered, died, was buried and rose again, not for the sake of humanity in a general way, but for the sake of each and every person in this humanity.

On this point, the great Russian Saint Tikhon of Zadonsk (1724–1783) wrote saying:

> You were sold and betrayed that I might be freed, I who was enslaved… You submitted to an unjust trial—You Who are the Judge of all the earth—that I might be freed from eternal judgement. You were made naked in order to clothe me in the robes of salvation, in the garments of

THE LORD JESUS WAS CRUCIFIED FOR MY SAKE

gladness. You were crowned with thorns that I might receive the crown of life… You were laid in the tomb that I might rise from the tomb… This You have done for me, Your servant, O my Lord!'[81]

We cannot fully comprehend the meaning of the Cross and the Resurrection until we understand that what Christ did was for us and for every one of us in particular.

It happened one Good Friday that three lost youths passed by a church in Paris. They noticed a long line of believers standing to make confession before the priest of that church. From their lack of faith, these three youths began to mock the believers, regarding all that happened on that day—the Friday of the Crucifixion—as nothing but a historical comedy play.

One of them decided to go into the church to tell the priest what he thought about Christ and Christianity. When he appeared before the confession father, he said to him, 'We were passing by outside the church and saw this great mass of people waiting to give their confessions. It seemed to us that everything that happens here is nothing but a comic play, and decided to come in and tell you what we thought.'

The priest replied, 'Good, but I ask one thing of you before you leave the church. Go into the nave and stand

---

[81] Tikhon of Zadonsk, 'Confession and Thanksgiving to Christ', trans. Helen Iswolsky, in G. P. Gedotov (ed.), *The Way of a Pilgrim and Other Classics of Russian Spirituality* (Mineola, NY: Dover, 1965): 222.

before the main sanctuary. Look up at Jesus hanging on the Cross and say to Him, "You died for my sake, O Christ, but it means nothing to me at all." I want you to repeat that sentence three times; then you can leave the church.'

The lost youth agreed and approached the sanctuary and looked upon the body of Christ hanging on the Cross, and with difficulty, said the first time: 'You died for my sake...'. He then turned and ran from the sanctuary.

The priest stopped him and said, 'You promised me you would say it three times.' So the youth went back hesitantly, and looked up at Christ. The words evaporated from his lips, but eventually he managed to say: 'You died for my sake...', before moving suddenly away from the sanctuary in fright.

The priest stopped him again and said, 'You promised you would say it three times.' With great reluctance the youth went back and lifted his gaze to the Cross, contemplating the wounds of the Crucified One for a long time.

He then returned to the priest and said, 'Father, I am ready to make my confession.'

Who can look at the Lord Jesus who was crucified for our sake and not say to Him, 'Have mercy on me Lord, for I am a sinner'?[82]

---

[82] Cf. Anthony M. Coniaris, *Orthodoxy: A Creed for Today* (Minneapolis, MN: Light & Life, 1972): 131–2.

THE LORD JESUS WAS CRUCIFIED FOR MY SAKE

A Message of Love

The Cross is not only true in itself, but something from which we can draw out another great truth, namely, the love of God for humanity: 'For God so loved the world that He gave His only begotten Son, that whoever believes in Him should not perish but have everlasting life' (John 3:16). God was no longer silent, no longer hidden far away from our cries, as He was in the past: 'Truly You are God, who hide Yourself, O God of Israel, the Saviour!' (Isa. 45:15). He has shone forth from His hiddenness and revealed His love from atop the Cross.

> But God demonstrates His own love toward us, in that while we were still sinners, Christ died for us (Rom. 5:8).
>
> In this is love, not that we loved God, but that He loved us and sent His Son to be the propitiation for our sins (1 John 4:10).
>
> Surely He has borne our griefs and carried our sorrows; yet we esteemed Him stricken, smitten by God, and afflicted. But He was wounded for our transgressions, He was bruised for our iniquities; the chastisement for our peace was upon Him, And by His stripes we are healed (Isa. 53:4–5).
>
> The Son of Man did not come to be served, but to serve, and to give His life a ransom for many (Matt. 20:28).
>
> Knowing that you were not redeemed with corruptible things, like silver or gold, from your aimless conduct received by tradition from your fathers, but with the precious blood of Christ (1 Pet. 1:18–19).

> In Him we have redemption through His blood, the forgiveness of sins, according to the riches of His grace (Eph. 1:7).
>
> Thereafter You did shine upon us as a good God and lover of mankind, and desired to save us from our captor. You desired to lead us once more into the Paradise of Joy. You sent Your prophets, but they could not save us. You gave the Law, but it did not become a help to us. You were pleased of Your own will to offer Yourself up to Death for our sake and for the life of the world.[83]

A priest once went to visit a dying man. There was no chance that he would be able to listen to a sermon before he passed away, and so the priest had no option except to hold up his cross—on which there was an image of the Crucified One. He brought the cross close to the sick man's eyes and said to him: 'See how great is God's love for you!'?

When the Lord Jesus died on the Cross, it was though He was saying to us: 'Nothing you can do to Me is capable of stopping My love for you. You can strike Me and crush Me and flog Me, and You can murder Me on the Cross, but I will never cease loving you. Such is the greatness of My love for you: "Father forgive them."'

Everything that took place on Golgotha was a window through which we can behold a loving heart suffering for our sake. Man indeed offered many sacrifices

---

[83] Anba Epiphanius (ed.), *Ḥūlāǧī al-Dayr al-Abiyaḍ* (Euchologion of the White Monastery) (Cairo: Madrasat al-Iskandariyya, 2014): 110.

THE LORD JESUS WAS CRUCIFIED FOR MY SAKE

to God over many centuries, but on Golgotha we behold God offering Himself as a redeeming sacrifice for man, for 'Greater love has no one than this, than to lay down one's life for his friends' (John 15:13). This is God's love for each one of us.

Does He Love Me?

A servant recalled: 'The happiest man I ever knew broke his spine at the age of 15 when he fell onto his back, and was bedridden for forty years. Not a day passed in all those years in which agonising pains did not struck him whenever he tried to move.

One day, one of the people tending to him asked this question: 'Does the Devil never fight against you, prompting you to doubt God and suggesting that He is cruel?' He responded automatically, 'Yes, he has tried that many times. When I used to sit and see my old school-friends driving their cars, the Devil would whisper to me, "If God is good, why has he left you here bedridden for so many years? You might have been a rich man by now, driving an expensive car!". And whenever I saw a friend of mine from childhood walking around in perfect health, the Devil would whisper in my ear: "If God loved you, wouldn't He be able to protect you from this cruel fate?"' When they asked him, 'How do you respond to the Devil about these temptations?' he answered immediately, 'I take him to Golgotha and show him Jesus. I point to the cruel wounds in

ANBA EPIPHANIUS

His hands and feet and side, and say to him, "Is there any love greater than this?"[84]

YOU ARE PRECIOUS IN GOD'S EYES

As the Cross reveals God's love for us, it also shows how dear you are in the eyes of God. If a man offers his life for your sake, you must certainly be an important person. If the man in question is God Himself, then you must be very important indeed. Just as we judge the value of artworks by the price they are appraised at, we can determine our own value by the price God paid to redeem us:

> Knowing that you were not redeemed with corruptible things, like silver or gold, from your aimless conduct received by tradition from your fathers, but with the precious blood of Christ (1 Pet. 1:18–19).

A child went to church for the first time on Good Friday. There, he listened attentively to the story of the Crucified Lord Jesus, and the extent of His great love for us, how He suffered for our sake, and how He forgave our sins and granted us eternal life! At the end of the Good Friday service, the worshippers began to make their way home. The child could not understand why the worshippers seemed so indifferent about what they had just heard. He sat on his seat and began to cry and sob. His father came up to him and said, 'My son, you must not let yourself be moved so much, or let this

---

[84] Cf. Anthony Coniaris, *Orthodoxy: A Creed for Today* (Minneapolis, MN: Light & Life Publishing, 1972): 134.

dominate your life, or else people will think you are immature.'[85]

It seems that the same thing sometimes happens with us when we attend the prayers of this great day year after year. We leave church as though we have just seen a Good Friday play, not realising the value of the great redemption that Christ accomplished for our sake, or the value of the love which compelled Him to give Himself up for us:

> But now in Christ Jesus you who once were far off have been brought near by the blood of Christ. For He Himself is our peace, who has made both one [the Jews and the Gentiles]… so as to create in Himself one new man from the two, thus making peace, and that He might reconcile them both to God in one body through the Cross, thereby putting to death the enmity (Eph. 2:13–16).

---

[85] Cf. *Ibid.*, 146.

TRUE JOY SPRINGS OUT OF THE EMPTY TOMB

Rejoice in the Lord (Phi. 3:1)

When Christ's body was laid in the tomb, sorrow settled upon the disciples and their hearts were filled with despair. They gathered in the upper room to weep over their terrible misfortune and hide from the oppression of the Jews. While they were still drowning in their sorrow, the Lord Jesus Himself appeared in their midst, showed them His hands and His feet, and preached to them of His Resurrection from the dead, and His trampling down death; and thus 'the disciples were glad when they saw the Lord' (John 20:20).

This gladness at the sight of the Lord and being in His presence was also experienced by St Paul, and so he implored the Philippians: 'Rejoice in the Lord always. Again I will say, rejoice!' (Phil. 4:4). The Greek word for joy, *chará*, and its verb form *chaírō* is repeated many times in the epistle to the Philippians to the extent that the epistle has been called, 'The Epistle of Joy'.

In ancient Greek literature, the word joy (*chará*) described the state of delight or pleasure felt by a woman at occasions such as childbirth, weddings and feasts. The expression *chaíre* was used as a greeting in everyday encounters, and as the opening term of an address in letters and writings, often translated as *Peace* or *Be well!*

Greek philosophers, especially the Stoics, thought human emotions could be divided into four categories: fears, desires, griefs and pleasures. Joy was considered one of the pleasures.[86] Even though they viewed these emotions as a passive response to an active impulse, they nonetheless considered joy to be a healthy phenomenon. While the Holy Scripture is not opposed to this perspective, it always connects joy with God.

Thus, the people rejoiced when God saved them from their enemies (cf. 1 Sam. 18:6), or when He granted them victory in battle (cf. Ps. 21). But the joy felt in worship was of a different sort. God rejoices in His people, granting them His good things (cf. Deut. 30:9; Ps. 147:11), and the people respond to this joy with praise, jubilation, hymns, and songs of joy (cf. Ps. 33:11; 95:1–2). Even the presentation of sacrifices in the Temple were accompanied with feelings of joy (cf. Deut. 12:12); thus, the yearly religious feasts were set up as 'days of joy' (Num. 10:10; Deut. 16:11).

Joy was an expression of a person's relationship with God. The righteous man's delight was in the law of God (cf. Ps 1:2; 119:14) or in His word (cf. Jer. 15:16). So also, joy was the reward for trusting in God and relying upon

---

[86] TN: On the four Stoic emotions, see Tad Brennan, "Stoic Moral Psychology" in *The Cambridge Companion to the Stoics*, ed. Brad Inwood (Cambridge: Cambridge University Press, 2003): 269–79.

TRUE JOY SPRINGS OUT OF THE EMPTY TOMB

Him: 'But he who trusts in the Lord, mercy shall surround him. Be glad in the Lord and rejoice, you righteous; and shout for joy, all you upright in heart!' (Ps. 32:10–11).

True joy, for the prophets of the Old Testament—especially those of the exile—was joy at the Messiah's coming, His restoration of the Kingdom of David, and His transformation of desolate places into fertile valleys (cf. Isa. 12:3, 6; 51:3). When God comes down among His people, there will be everlasting joy (cf. Isa. 51:11). What the prophets saw and hoped for became a reality at the coming of the Messiah, the Lord Jesus. The people experienced true joy at God's coming down to be among His people: '"Sing and rejoice, O daughter of Zion! For behold, I am coming and I will dwell in your midst," says the Lord' (Zech. 2:10). Joy became one of the basic features accompanying Christ's life on the earth: joy at His birth (cf. Luke 19:6), joy at His Resurrection (cf. Matt. 28:8) and joy at His return to the Father (cf. Luke 24:52). Christ's life on the earth was like a wedding feast; Christ was the bridegroom, and His disciples the children of the wedding rejoicing with the bridegroom in their midst.

Joy was also a feature of His teaching and preaching. He likened the Kingdom of Heaven to the joy experienced by a man who discovers a hidden treasure (cf. Matt. 13:44). The salvation of God is likened to the joy of a shepherd who finds his lost sheep (cf. Luke 15:5–7), or that of a woman who finds a lost coin (cf. Luke 15:9–

10). How much greater is the Father's joy when He finds His lost child (cf. Luke 15:32)! In all these situations, a call goes out to friends and relatives to share in this joy. The joy that accompanies God's gift of salvation must necessarily spread to those nearby until it is shared by all. Even heaven and the angels rejoice when salvation is effected (cf. Luke 15:10).

When Lord Jesus was with the disciples in the upper room, He promised them a perfect joy that could never be taken away from them even by tribulations (cf. John 15:11, 16, 24; 17:13). He promised them joy in the salvation they would receive through the Lord's Death and Resurrection. This is true and perfect joy is a theme of the New Testament: joy in the person of the Lord Jesus Christ, 'whom having not seen you love. Though now you do not see Him, yet believing, you rejoice with joy inexpressible and full of glory…' (1 Pet. 1:8); joy that our names are written in heaven (cf. Luke 10:20); joy at partaking in the wedding supper of the Lamb (cf. Rev. 19:7); joy at hearing the voice of the Lord saying, 'Well done good and faithful servant' (Matt. 25:21).

This joy was also embodied in the early Church as seen in the Acts of the Apostles. The Samaritans rejoiced with great joy when they believed in the message of salvation (cf. Acts 8:8); the Ethiopian eunuch went on his way with joy when he had received baptism at the hands of Philip the Deacon (cf. 8:39); and the people of Antioch rejoiced and glorified God when the Apostle Paul preached the message of salvation to them (cf. 13:48).

TRUE JOY SPRINGS OUT OF THE EMPTY TOMB

Joy in Tribulations

Joy in tribulations is another kind of joy experienced by the early Christians. The Lord Jesus blessed those who were persecuted for righteousness' sake and advised them to rejoice because their reward was great in heaven (cf. Matt. 5:11–12). The apostles attained this blessing, for when the Jews beat them for preaching Christ, 'they departed from the presence of the council, rejoicing that they were counted worthy to suffer shame for His name' (Acts 5:41). In the epistle to the Hebrews, we see Christians experiencing joy even when they were deprived of their possessions, knowing that they had a better and an enduring possession in heaven (cf. Heb. 10:34). St Peter urged Christians to rejoice in the sufferings of Christ so that they may also rejoice in the revelation of His glory (1 Pet. 4:12–14); for St James, falling into trials leads to 'all joy' (James 1:2).

But it is St Paul who most insists upon this paradox of joy in suffering. He saw his sufferings as a partaking in the sufferings of Christ: 'I now rejoice in my sufferings for you, and fill up in my flesh what is lacking in the afflictions of Christ' (Col. 1:24). His sufferings always reminded him of the Lord's grace, that is, the power of Christ working in his weakness (cf. 2 Cor. 12:9). The Greek word for grace—*cháris*—is a derivative of the word for joy, *chará*. Therefore, the grace of Christ is the gift that transforms our sufferings into joy, and causes us to experience complete joy even in the most severe trials and tribulations.

We see this clearly in the joyful epistle St Paul sent to the people of Philippi, in which he calls on them to rejoice always. Even though he was suffering from those false brethren who were 'adding affliction to his chains', he says nonetheless: 'In this I rejoice, yes, and will rejoice' (Phil. 1:16–17). In addition, although he had been cast into prison awaiting trial, not knowing whether he would be set free or sentenced to death, we hear him say all the same: 'Rejoice in the Lord always. Again I will say, rejoice!' (4:4). The church of Philippi itself was suffering from griefs and dissensions (cf. 2:1–12; 4:2–3); the unity of the church was in peril. So long as there was division in the Church, the Holy Spirit, Who is the Spirit of unity, would not be at work in their community, and as a consequence, one of the gifts of the Holy Spirit would disappear from among them: namely, joy (Gal. 5:22). For this reason, we find Paul exhorting them saying, 'Fulfill my joy by being like-minded, having the same love, being of one accord, of one mind' (Phil. 2:2). In all these circumstances, the joy St Paul has in mind is true joy in the Lord Jesus: 'Finally, my brethren, rejoice in the Lord' (Phil. 3:1).

This joy experienced by the early Christians—which the Church continues to live by to this day, even as she undergoes trials, tribulations and persecutions—is a fruit of the Resurrection of the Lord from the dead, after He had taken upon Himself all the weaknesses and emotions of human beings—grief, anxiety, pain and hatred—in order to transform them for us and for our sake into joy,

TRUE JOY SPRINGS OUT OF THE EMPTY TOMB

peace, meekness and patience. Accordingly, the Church exhorts her children in the Canon of the Resurrection[87], saying:

> Come all you faithful, let us worship the Resurrection of Christ. For behold, through His Cross, joy has entered into the whole world.

The same hymn addresses the Virgin:

> You gave birth, O Virgin, to the Giver of Life. He saved Adam from sin and granted Eve joy in place of sadness. He granted us life and salvation from corruption and change.

It then addresses to the Marys standing outside the tomb:

> The time for weeping is over, do not weep but preach the Resurrection to the apostles.

Indeed, the Lord's Incarnation was the first entrance of true joy into the world, and this joy became complete at His Resurrection from the dead.

On the feast of the Annunciation, St Gregory the Thaumaturgus sings:

> Today strains of praise are sung joyfully
> by the choir of angels,
> And the light of the advent of Christ
> shines brightly upon the faithful.
> Today is the glad spring-time to us,
> and Christ the Sun of Righteousness
> Has beamed with clear light around us,

---

[87] TN: *Tennav* or the Hymn of the Resurrection from the Midnight Praises of the Resurrection.

and illumined the minds of the faithful.
Today Adam is made anew,
And moves in the choir of angels,
having winged his way to heaven.
Today the whole circle of the earth is filled with joy,
Since the sojourn of the Holy Spirit
has come upon men (Lk 1:35).
Today the grace of God and the hope of the unseen
Shine through all wonders transcending imagination,
And reveals the mystery
that was kept hidden from eternity...
Today the word of David is fulfilled:
'Let the heavens rejoice, and let the earth be glad.
The fields shall be joyful, and all the trees of the wood,
Before the Lord, for He is coming'
(Ps 95. [LXX]:11–13).[88]

St Cyril the Great also contemplates on what the Lord said to the Marys after the Resurrection: 'Rejoice!' *chaírete* (Matt. 28:9):

> The women having been taught the mystery by the voice of angels, run to tell these things to the disciples. For it was fitting that this grace, though so splendid, should be granted to women. For she who of old was the minister of death is now freed from her guilt by ministering to the voice of the holy angels, and by being the first both to learn and tell the adorable mystery of the Resurrection. The female sex therefore gained both acquittal from their reproach and the reversal of their curse. For He Who of

---

[88] Gregory Thaumaturgus, *First Homily on the Annunciation* (ANF 6:58). Lightly modernised.

TRUE JOY SPRINGS OUT OF THE EMPTY TOMB

old had said to them, 'In pains shall you bear children,' gave them deliverance from their misfortune, by having met them in the garden, as another Evangelist mentions, and said, 'Rejoice!' (Matt. 28:9).[89]

---

[89] Cf. Cyril of Alexandria, *Commentary on Luke, Sermon* 153, trans. R. Payne Smith (Oxford: Oxford University Press, 1859), 724–5.

THE GIFTS OF THE HOLY SPIRIT

The descent of the Holy Spirit upon the disciples on the day of Pentecost was accompanied by the appearance of many spiritual gifts which had not previously been present. The most apparent and the most frequently questioned of these was the gift of speaking in tongues, i.e. the ability to speak in new languages which the speaker does not know, but which the Holy Spirit utters through his mouth.

The New Testament uses a range of words translated into modern languages as *gift*. The most common and frequently used is *chárisma*, meaning a free gift, a gift given without reciprocation. This is the word used to describe the charismatic movements which have appeared in the West in recent years. It is usually employed to describe the special, immaterial power of God which works within a believing person, enabling them to speak or serve within the church. This word appears 17 times in the New Testament.

There is another important word translated as 'spiritual gifts' which is *pneumatiká*, from the Greek word for spirit (*pnéuma*), which means spiritual things, or things of the spirit. It is used in this way in 1 Cor. 12:1 and 14:1, where it bears exactly the same meaning as *chárisma*: 'Now concerning spiritual gifts [*pneumatikōn*] brethren, I do not want you to be ignorant' (1 Cor. 12:1) and 'Pursue love, and desire spiritual gifts [*pneumatiká*], but especially that you may prophesy' (1 Cor. 14:1).

Reflecting on these two words, we find that a gift is first a thing given freely, and then, a spiritual gift, particularly related to the Holy Spirit.[90]

One of the most significant discussions of spiritual gifts takes place in 1 Corinthians 12–14. In these chapters, the Apostle Paul addresses the issue of ignorance about these gifts, and also, the issue of their misuse among the Corinthians. St Paul explains that the usefulness of these gifts is primarily for the advantage of believers: "But the manifestation of the Spirit is given to each one for the profit of all" (1 Cor. 12:7). Then, for the edification of the Church: 'Even so you, since you are zealous for spiritual gifts, let it be for the edification of the church that you seek to excel' (1 Cor. 14:12). So the fundamental value of spiritual gifts is for the faithful to benefit from each other by ministering to one another: 'As each one has received a gift, minister it to one another, as good stewards of the manifold grace of God' (1 Pet. 4:1); this will lead to 'the edifying of the body of Christ' (Eph. 4:12), so that 'in all things God may be glorified' (1 Pet. 4:11).

Thus, spiritual gifts benefit the community of the faithful, edifying the community, glorifying God, and unifying the believers more and more as members of the one body of Christ: 'For as the body is one and has many

---

[90] Cf. Kindell H. Easley, 'The Gifts of the Holy Spirit', *Biblical Illustrator* 3 (1991): 61.

THE GIFTS OF THE HOLY SPIRIT

members, but all the members of that one body, being many, are one body, so also is Christ' (1 Cor. 12:12). Because of this strong focus on the unity of Christ's body in these chapters, we are struck when we hear of 'spiritual gifts' which lead to divisions in the Church or the confusion and disturbance of her members.

Spiritual Gifts and the Fruits of the Spirit

St Paul speaks also about the nature of spiritual gifts, and how they differ from the fruits of the Spirit. In his letter to the Galatians, he mentions nine fruits of the Holy Spirit: 'love, joy, peace, longsuffering, kindness, goodness, faithfulness, gentleness, self-control' (Gal. 5:22–3). It is clear that all Christians who have received the gift of the Holy Spirit are obliged to grow in all these fruits. These fruits are abiding and eternal, but spiritual gifts are provisional and will have an end: 'Love never fails. But whether there are prophecies, they will fail; whether there are tongues, they will cease; whether there is knowledge, it will vanish away… And now abide faith, hope, love' (1 Cor. 13:8, 13).

The fruits of the Spirit are a necessity for every Christian to strive for and develop. But spiritual gifts are different. No one receives all the gifts: 'Do all have gifts of healings? Do all speak with tongues? Do all interpret?' (1 Cor. 12:30). Nor does anyone choose for himself the gift he is to obtain. For it is the Holy Spirit Who chooses the gift, 'distributing to each one individually as He wills' (1 Cor. 12:11).

These gifts can be falsified if some people are inwardly puffed up or deluded, relying on their own natural capacities; the demons can even help them along and deceive them in this. In this way, they lose their eternity, and the Lord Jesus says of them: 'Many will say to Me in that day, "Lord, Lord, have we not prophesied in Your name, cast out demons in Your name, and done many wonders in Your name?" And then I will declare to them, "I never knew you; depart from Me, you who practice lawlessness!"' (Matt. 7:22–3).

And no wonder, 'For Satan himself transforms himself into an angel of light' (2 Cor. 11:14), 'For they are spirits of demons, performing signs, which go out to the kings of the earth' (Rev. 16:14).

It is clear therefore that it is the fruits of the Holy Spirit, their work and their service—not the spiritual gifts—which are the sure indication of the Holy Spirit's indwelling a person.

Spiritual Gifts and Natural Gifts

The gifts of the Spirit differ from natural gifts. Natural gifts are the innate or created capacities which God gives to a person from his or her fleshly birth, such as talents in athletics, music, and so on. But the gifts of the Spirit are given by the Holy Spirit as in the day of Pentecost, in a very particular manner. St Paul says, 'But one and the same Spirit works all these things, distributing to each one individually as He wills… For by one Spirit we were all baptized into one body—whether Jews or

THE GIFTS OF THE HOLY SPIRIT

Greeks, whether slaves or free—and have all been made to drink into one Spirit' (1 Cor. 12:11, 13).

Spiritual gifts do not clash with natural gifts; the two can co-exist, and the Spirit can work through a person's natural gifts, causing them to grow and granting them capacities which were not there before. So also, a person might receive spiritual gifts which make him capable of things that were not previously possible, for instance: the gift of speaking in tongues on the day of Pentecost (Acts 2:4), and the gift of preaching in the name of Christ which St Paul received as soon as he converted to Christianity (Acts 9:20–22), or the amazing and abundant gifts of wonder-working and healing which the apostles received. Accordingly, St Paul declares that spiritual gifts which violate the laws of nature—such as the working of 'signs and wonders and mighty deeds' (2 Cor. 12:12)—are among the distinguishing marks of an apostle.

As for those gifts which do not seem to violate nature, such as gifts of service, preaching, charity or administration (Rom. 12:6–8), the Holy Spirit can give them to a person in one of two ways.

First, if a person lacks any natural gifts suitable for edifying the Church, the Spirit grants them gifts which enable them to work for the Church's edification. We have an example of this in our Fathers the apostles, who were mostly of ordinary stock, but who, after the coming down upon them of the Holy Spirit, became teachers of the whole world: 'Now when they saw the boldness of Peter and John, and perceived that they were uneducated and untrained men, they marvelled. And they realized that they had been with Jesus' (Acts 4:13).

Second, if a person has natural gifts and abilities, the Holy Spirit amplifies them and puts them to work for the Kingdom of God. A good example of this is St Paul the Apostle, who was steeped in Jewish learning, zealous for the teachings of the Fathers: 'I am indeed a Jew, born in Tarsus of Cilicia, but brought up in this city at the feet of Gamaliel, taught according to the strictness of our Fathers' law, and was zealous toward God as you all are today' (Acts 22:3). The Holy Spirit made use of him after he believed, seeing that he was a chosen vessel for the preaching of the Gospel:

> Then Ananias answered, "Lord, I have heard from many about this man, how much harm he has done to Your saints in Jerusalem. And here he has authority from the chief priests to bind all who call on Your name." But the Lord said to him, "Go, for he is a chosen vessel of Mine to bear My name before Gentiles, kings, and the children of Israel. For I will show him how many things he must suffer for My name's sake" (Acts 9:13–16).

THE HOLY SPIRIT: GIVER OF GIFTS

In his first letter to the Corinthians (1 Cor. 12:7–11), St Paul declares six times that the Holy Spirit is the one who grants spiritual gifts, and that the Holy Spirit is the one who determines which gifts are given to a person: 'But one and the same Spirit works all these things, distributing to each one individually as He wills' (1 Cor.

THE GIFTS OF THE HOLY SPIRIT

12:11). The Holy Spirit does not grant His gifts while keeping Himself at a distance, but rather through a state of coming down or indwelling. What are spiritual gifts other than the effects of the descent of the Holy Spirit? 'But you shall receive power when the Holy Spirit has come upon you; and you shall be witnesses to Me' (Acts 1:8). The Holy Spirit descends into our beings granting us His gifts: 'But the anointing which you have received from Him abides in you, and you do not need that anyone teach you; but as the same anointing teaches you concerning all things, and is true, and is not a lie' (1 John 2:27). This is to say that when the Holy Spirit comes down and dwells within a person, He begins to work His works and bestow His powers: 'But if the Spirit of Him who raised Jesus from the dead *dwells in you*, He who raised Christ from the dead will also give life to your mortal bodies *through His Spirit who dwells in you*' (Rom. 8:11).

Who Has the Gifts?

How many Christians possess the gifts of the Spirit? According to the writings of the Apostles Peter and Paul, all Christians possess the gifts of the Holy Spirit. St Paul says, 'But the manifestation of the Spirit is given *to each one* for the profit of all ... But one and the same Spirit works all these things, distributing *to each one* individually as He wills' (1 Cor. 12:7, 11). And St Peter says, 'As *each one* has received a gift, minister it to one another, as good stewards of the manifold grace of God' (1 Pet. 4:10). If in the early Church was given to every member to inherit the gifts of the Spirit, why do so few among us seem to have them today? The answer is that the gift needs to be kindled:

> Do not neglect the gift that is in you, which was given to you by prophecy with the laying on of the hands of the eldership. Meditate on these things; give yourself entirely to them, that your progress may be evident to all. Take heed to yourself and to the doctrine. Continue in them, for in doing this you will save both yourself and those who hear you (1 Tim. 4:14–16).

St Paul repeats his commandment to his disciple Timothy once more, saying:

> Therefore I remind you to stir up the gift of God which is in you through the laying on of my hands. For God has not given us a spirit of fear, but of power and of love and of a sound mind (2 Tim. 1:6–7).

From St Paul's two letters to his disciple Timothy, we clearly see the necessity of obedience and submission to spiritual fathers, and the need for their advice, guidance, and counsel in order to grow these gifts and make use of them for the edification of the Church and the glory of Christ. Also, those who quench the Holy Spirit, or grieve Him by breaking God's commandments or follow their desires make it impossible for the Spirit to work His gifts in them.

Diversities of Gifts

St Paul states that there are many spiritual gifts—'There are diversities of gifts, but the same Spirit' (1 Cor.

THE GIFTS OF THE HOLY SPIRIT

12:4)—but he does not enumerate them all. He discusses these gifts in four places spread throughout his epistles. In 1 Cor. 12:8–10, he mentions nine gifts:

> For to one is given the word of *wisdom*, to another the word of *knowledge*, to another *faith*, to another *gifts of healings*, to another the *working of miracles*, to another *prophecy*, to another *discerning of spirits*, to another *different kinds of tongues*, to another the *interpretation of tongues*.

In 1 Cor. 12:28–30, he mentions eight gifts, including four new gifts not found among the previous nine:

> And God has appointed these in the church: first *apostles*, second prophets, third *teachers*, after that miracles, then gifts of healings, *helps*, *administrations*, varieties of tongues.

In the letter to the Romans, he mentions seven gifts, four of them new:

> Having then gifts differing according to the grace that is given to us, let us use them: if *prophecy*, let us prophesy in proportion to our faith; or *ministry*, let us use it in our *ministering*; he who teaches, in *teaching*; he who *exhorts*, in exhortation; he who *gives*, with liberality; he who *leads*, with diligence; he who *shows mercy*, with cheerfulness (Rom. 12:6–8).

Finally, in the letter to Ephesus, he mentions five gifts, of which two are new: 'And He Himself gave some to be apostles, some prophets, some *evangelists*, and some *pastors* and teachers' (Eph. 4:11). Of course, the Spirit would be able to add any number of gifts not mentioned here.

These gifts can be divided into two general categories: gifts of action or service, and gifts of speaking. St Peter sets a condition on the use of all these gifts:

> If anyone speaks, let him speak as the oracles of God. If anyone ministers, let him do it as with the ability which God supplies, that in all things God may be glorified through Jesus Christ (1 Pet. 4:11).

The Gifts Today

Are all these gifts still granted to believers in our time? The same Holy Spirit who was at work in the early Church is at work in the Church now. However, in the early Church, there was a need for special gifts which appeared openly and powerfully, like speaking in tongues, in order to help the apostles and preachers to preach the Gospel by word to different nations and to confirm their preaching by signs and wonders.

These gifts did not cease after the time of the early Church. Many of the early Desert Fathers received the gift of speaking in other languages for the benefit of those who came to them seeking the salvation of their souls, as happened with Abba Macarius and Abba Pachomius. This gift still appears in the Church from time to time.

There is no doubt that the Holy Spirit is still able even now to grant believers new gifts to meet the needs of today's Church; however, the Spirit first requires sincere souls and prepared vessels to receive Him. We do not pray to receive the gifts; it is rather the Holy Spirit who grants them to each one as He wills. But we do pray that

THE GIFTS OF THE HOLY SPIRIT

God give us the Holy Spirit according to His blessed promise: '[He will] give the Holy Spirit to those who ask Him' (Lk 11:13). May God grant us to be filled with the fruits of the Spirit, and that God may keep the bearers of the gifts from being lost, and that the gift may be used to edify the Church to the glory of God in Jesus Christ our Lord.

In his book *Against the Heresies*, St Irenaeus explains how the gift is given by the Holy Spirit, and how the gift needs the Church if it is to grow:

> For this gift of God (*the Holy Spirit*) has been entrusted to the Church, as breath was to the first created man, for this purpose, that all the members receiving it may be vivified; and the [means of] communion with Christ has been distributed throughout it, that is, the Holy Spirit, the earnest of incorruption, the means of confirming our faith, and the ladder of ascent to God ... For where the Church is, there is the Spirit of God; and where the Spirit of God is, there is the Church, and every kind of grace; but the Spirit is truth. Those, therefore, who do not partake of Him, are neither nourished into life from the mother's breasts, nor do they enjoy that most limpid fountain which issues from the body of Christ.[91]

---

[91] Irenaeus of Lyons, *Against Heresies* 3.24.1 (ANF 1:458).

CHILDREN OF GOD

One of the most sublime and powerful concepts to be found in Holy Scripture is that the eternal God, Creator of the universe and everything in it, was pleased to call sinful, dust-formed human beings His own children. The Bible expresses the idea of a human being becoming a child of God in several ways. One of these ways centres around the concept of *adoption*.

The word adoption, *hyiothesía*, occurs five times in the New Testament, all in the letters of St Paul. Paul uses this word without explanation or comment, knowing that his audience will understand what he means by it.

Adoption in the Old Testament:

It is a rarity to find the concept of adoption in the Old Testament. There was no expression in the Hebrew language to refer to adoption, nor is there any statute governing adoption to be found among the laws of the Old Testament. Perhaps this is because the Israelites had ways of dealing with the problem of not being able to conceive children other than adoption. It was acceptable to marry more than one wife, and a brother could marry his brother's widow to raise up children for his brother (cf. Deut. 25:5–10). These reduced the need for the practice of adoption. The Law also stipulated that inheritance should remain within the one tribe, and forbade the transfer of inheritance out of a tribe (cf. Lev 25:23); this calmed the anxieties of married couples who had no descendants.[92]

Nonetheless, by studying the adoption customs prevalent in Syria and Mesopotamia, we can shed some light on the few cases of adoption that occur in the Old Testament. In the ancient Middle East, adoption was sanctioned by law, such that a person could be taken into a new family other than his own and enjoy all the benefits and responsibilities of a natural child. Applying this principle to the Old Testament, we can identify a small number of cases where adoption takes place, such as Abraham the father of fathers' adoption of Eliezer the Damascene (cf. Gen. 15:3), Pharaoh's daughter's adoption of Moses (cf. Ex. 2:16), Mordecai's adoption of Esther (cf. Est. 2:7, 15) and possibly the Egyptian Queen Tahpenes' adoption of Genubath (cf. 1 Kings 11:20).

Adoption in the Old Testament also has a spiritual connotation. God considered Israel as His son, even though the Israelites did not honour the duties of their sonship:

> I have nourished and brought up children, and they have rebelled against Me; the ox knows its owner and the donkey its master's crib, but Israel does not know, My people do not consider (Isa. 1:2–3).

---

[92] Cf. Charles F. D. Moule, "Adoption," in *The Interpreter's Dictionary of the Bible*, Vol. I (Nashville: Abingdon, 1981): 48.

CHILDREN OF GOD

God's main wish in designating Israel as His child was for Israel to hold fast to this sonship, not to deny it or turn their back on God's fatherhood:

> But I said: "How can I put you among the children and give you a pleasant land, a beautiful heritage of the hosts of nations?" "And I said: 'You shall call Me, "My Father," and not turn away from Me.'" (Jer. 3:19)

In addition, the Lord says, 'Israel is My son, My firstborn' (Ex. 4:22), and again, 'For I am a Father to Israel, and Ephraim is My firstborn' (Jer. 31:9).

The fatherhood of God also appears in God's choosing of the king who is to come from the line of David to be called the Son of God:

> He shall cry to Me,
> "You are my Father,
> My God, and the rock of my salvation."
> Also I will make him My firstborn,
> the highest of the kings of the earth.
> My mercy I will keep for him forever,
> and My covenant shall stand firm with him.
> His seed also I will make to endure forever,
> and his throne as the days of heaven (Ps. 89:26–29).

We may note here that this divine act of election supports the Apostle Paul's words about the children of Israel:

> …my countrymen according to the flesh, who are Israelites, to whom pertain the adoption, the glory, the covenants, the giving of the law, the service of God, and the promises (Rom. 9:3–4).

ANBA EPIPHANIUS

Adoption in the New Testament:

In apostolic times, the practice of adoption was widespread in the Greco-Roman world. Among the Greeks, an adoption would be announced in the public marketplace in front of all the citizens before the name of the adopted person was registered in the city's public record. It was a condition of adoption that the adopted person keep his name and the name of his family, as well as the gods he used to worship. Among the Romans, adoption was carried out when the father sold his child to a new father three times, after which the new father would appear before a judge and declare that this child had now become his son. In this way, the son became a legal heir to his father by adoption.[93]

From this, we realise that St Paul the Apostle was using a concept that would have been well-known to all his readers: in his letter to the Romans, he uses the word *adoption* (*hyiothesía*) to explain God's relation to the people of Israel and his election of them, as we saw earlier. In the four remaining places where Paul uses this word, it describes God's relationship to the new Israel, that is, those who believe in His Son Jesus Christ.

Adoption as a Spiritual Gift (Eph. 1:3–5)

St Paul did not choose the concept of *adoption* haphazardly; he wanted to make it clear that our sonship to God was not a natural sonship, but a spiritual gift granted to us by God. Nor did God turn to adoption as

---

[93] Cf. Eduard Schweizer, 'υἱοθεσία,' in *TDNT*, VIII: 398.

CHILDREN OF GOD

a last resort in the problem of humanity. The gift of adoption was in the mind of God before we were created, from eternity, and it is grounded in God's love for us in Christ Jesus:

> Blessed be the God and Father of our Lord Jesus Christ, who has blessed us with every spiritual blessing in the heavenly places in Christ, just as He chose us in Him before the foundation of the world, that we should be holy and without blame before Him in love, having predestined us to adoption as sons by Jesus Christ to Himself, according to the good pleasure of His will (Eph. 1:3–5).

St Cyril the Great explains this as follows:

> He humbled Himself that He might raise what is humble by nature to His own height; and He wore the form of a slave, even though He was by nature Lord and Son, that He might transfer what is a slave by nature into the glory of sonship, in conformity with his own likeness, like Him. Since He became like us (that is, a human being) in order that we might become like Him (I mean gods and sons), He receives our properties into Himself and He gives us His own in return... We ascend to honours above our nature by our likeness to Him, for though we are not sons by nature, we are called sons of God... By nature and in truth the God of all is the Father of Christ. When it comes to us, however, He is not our Father by nature, but rather our God, since He is Creator and Lord. But since the Son has mixed Himself with us, in a manner of speaking, He grants to our nature the honour that properly and strictly speaking belongs to Him when He refers to His own Father as our common Father. (John 20:17, 'My Father and

your Father').[94]

ADOPTION AND THE DIVINE INHERITANCE
(GAL. 4:4–7)

According to the Law and the statutes, a son who has not come of age cannot access his father's inheritance, but is under guardians (cf. Gal. 4:1). In this way, we were under the guardianship of the Law, having no right to call God our Father or to receive a heavenly inheritance. But at the time appointed by God—namely, when His Only-Begotten Son took flesh—God granted us adoption in the Lord Jesus Christ, making us heirs of God through Christ. Not only that, but God gave His Holy Spirit, through Whom we are able to cry out to God saying, 'Abba, Father!' The word *Abba* is an Aramaic word used by children to call their fathers:

> But when the fullness of the time had come, God sent forth His Son, born of a woman, born under the law, to redeem those who were under the law, that we might receive the adoption as sons. And because you are sons, God has sent forth the Spirit of His Son into your hearts, crying out, 'Abba, Father!' Therefore you are no longer a slave but a son, and if a son, then an heir of God through Christ (Gal. 4:4–7).

St Athanasius the Apostolic comments on this verse saying:

---

[94] Cyril of Alexandria, *Commentary on John*, II:12, 1, trans. David R. Maxwell, ed. Joel C. Elowsky (IVP Academic: Downers Grove, IL, 2013): 363.

CHILDREN OF GOD

But this is God's kindness to man, that of whom He is Maker, of them according to grace He afterwards becomes Father also; becomes, that is, when men, His creatures, receive into their hearts, as the Apostle says, 'the Spirit of His Son, crying, "Abba, Father."' He goes on to describe the heavenly inheritance we will receive, saying, 'The Word became flesh, that He might make man capable of Godhead.'[95]

Adoption and Deliverance from Slavery (Rom. 8:15–17)

In his letter to the Romans, St Paul confirms our adoption as children of God and our right to the heavenly inheritance, for before the Lord Christ's incarnation, we were ruled by the spirit of bondage and lived as slaves of sin. But after believing in Christ and the new birth of water and Spirit, we attained the spirit of adoption, the spirit of deliverance from sin and the power of darkness. As a result, it became possible for us to call God our Father, and we became heirs of God and heirs of Christ. Therefore, if at present we are subjected to the sufferings of this age, it will certainly lead to glory:

> For you did not receive the spirit of bondage again to fear, but you received the Spirit of adoption by whom we cry out, 'Abba, Father.' The Spirit Himself bears witness with our spirit that we are children of God, and if children, then heirs—heirs of God and joint heirs with Christ, if indeed we suffer with Him, that we may also be glorified together

---

[95] Athanasius of Alexandria, *Orations Against the Arians*, Oration 2,59 (*NPNF* 2/4: 380).

(Rom. 8:15–17).

St Cyril the Great sings of our deliverance from slavery to sonship, saying:

> What boundless generosity! What incomparable gentleness, befitting Him alone! He bestows upon us His own glory. He raises slaves to the dignity of freedom. He crowns man's estate with such honour as surpasses the power of nature. He brings that to pass which was spoken of old by the voice of the Psalmist: 'I said, You are gods: and all of you children of the Most High' (Ps. 81:6, LXX). For lo! He rescues us from the measure of slavery, bestowing upon us by His grace that which by nature we did not possess, and permits us to call God Father, as being admitted to the rank of sons.[96]

THE PERFECTION OF ADOPTION (ROM. 8:22–23)

Finally, and in the same epistle to the Romans, St Paul moves from his affirmation of the adoption which takes place now in an incomplete form to the coming adoption in its final form. For even though we are children of God, we are still subjected to various sufferings which cause us to groan and cry out until we attain adoption in its final form. The entire creation partakes of this groaning together with us, for it also is awaiting transfiguration in the final resurrection:

> For we know that the whole creation groans and labours with birth pangs together until now. Not only that, but

---

[96] Cyril of Alexandria, *Commentary on Luke*, Sermon 71, trans. R. Payne Smith (Oxford University Press, 1859): 325–6. Lightly modernised.

we also who have the firstfruits of the Spirit, even we ourselves groan within ourselves, eagerly waiting for the adoption, the redemption of our body (Rom. 8:22–3).

The redemption of the body refers to the final resurrection. Thus, the Christian, along with the whole creation, eagerly and patiently awaits the perfection and consummation of his relationship to God, when he or she will truly experience the fullness of what it means to be adopted by God. In this regard, St John the Theologian says:

> Behold what manner of love the Father has bestowed on us, that we should be called children of God!… Beloved, now we are children of God [i.e. *by adoption*]; and it has not yet been revealed what we shall be, but we know that when He is revealed, we shall be like Him, for we shall see Him as He is (1 John 3:1–2).

Therefore, when St Paul's uses the concept of adoption to describe our relationship with God, he puts in our minds several foundational realities which must be well-understood. First, adoption reminds us that we are not children of God by nature, but that our sonship is a gift from Him, and thus, we formerly had no rights before God as children. Second, our adoption by God rests on the basis of His election of us; He appointed us to adoption from before the foundation of the world. Third, our adoption by God was carried out through the Incarnation of the true Son of God, whereby we became children of God in Him, and entered into a relationship of love which casts out fear. Fourth, as children of God, we received a right to the inheritance of God. One day, we will experience the glory of this adoption in its fullest form.

SPIRITUAL UNDERSTANDING OF PHYSICAL TRAINING IN THE LETTERS OF ST PAUL

In ancient times, Greece was famous for its athletic games. The festivals and tournaments in which athletes competed held an important place in the life and thought of the Greek people. One of the most famous tournaments was held on the plain of Mount Olympus in honour of Zeus, the greatest of the Greek gods. This tournament later became known as the Olympic Games and was held every four years. In addition, there were three major tournaments held yearly in the main Greek cities.

The Apostle Paul was no stranger to this culture of athletic competition, for he was raised in the city of Tarsus, known for its Greek culture. He was quite comfortable using the language of athletic competition, which was familiar to his readers, as a means of conveying important spiritual truths. St Paul uses many athletic terms, particularly in his letters to the Corinthians and the Philippians, where the believers were Christians of Greek culture. He also uses terms like this in his two letters to his disciple Timothy, whose father had been Greek (cf. Acts 1:16).

One of St Paul's clearest use of this imagery is found in the first letter to Corinth:

ANBA EPIPHANIUS

Do you not know that those who run in a race all run, but one receives the prize? Run in such a way that you may obtain it. And everyone who competes for the prize is temperate in all things. Now they do it to obtain a perishable crown, but we for an imperishable crown. Therefore I run thus: not with uncertainty. Thus I fight: not as one who beats the air. But I discipline my body and bring it into subjection, lest, when I have preached to others, I myself should become disqualified. (1 Cor. 9:24–27)

'THOSE WHO RUN IN A RACE'

The word translated in this passage as 'race' is the Greek word *stádion*; the origin of the word 'stadium'. A stadium was originally a unit of measurement of length corresponding to roughly 600 Greek feet (625 Latin feet, 607 English feet, or 192 metres).[97] It measured the exact length of the arena in which the contestants competed at the Olympic tournament.

St Paul compared life to a race between a group of competitors in which the prize goes only to the winner. He was not saying that Christians are in competition with one another to attain a crown, but rather that even though all people—every human being—run in the race, a Christian has a particular obligation to run. He nonetheless encouraged Christian runners, stating that they could win the crown: 'Run in such a way that you may obtain it' (1 Cor. 9:24). The Apostle speaks boldly here because he is personally acquainted with the One who grants the crowns, and he is confident in His love,

---

[97] Cf. *GELNT*: 771.

wisdom and justice: 'For I know whom I have believed and am persuaded that He is able to keep what I have committed to Him until that Day' (2 Tim. 1:12).

The Apostle then offers insight from his own experience to every Christian, coaching them in the art of exerting oneself and racing on the spiritual plane, for 'everyone who competes for the prize is temperate in all things.' The verb compete (*agōnízomai*) here comes from a Greek root meaning to fight, struggle or sacrifice oneself to the best of one's ability. In a sporting context, it means to enter into a furious competition with someone.[98]

To be temperate—*enkrateúomai*, to keep oneself—refers to the period of preparation before a competition: a period as long as ten months in which all the athletes and judges would spend in training and strenuous exercise. On this period of preparation, the Stoic philosopher Epictetus said:

> You have to submit to discipline, follow a strict diet, give up sweet cakes, train under compulsion, at a fixed hour, in heat or in cold; you must not drink cold water, nor wine just whenever you feel like it.[99]

---

[98] Cf. *GELNT*: 15.

[99] Epictetus, *The Manual* (*Enchiridion*) 29. Cf. W. A. Oldfather (ed.), *The Discourses as Reported by Arrian, the Manual and Fragments*, vol. II, Loeb Classical Library (Cambridge, MA: Harvard University Press, 1956): 508.

Tertullian likens the life of Christian martyrs to Greek athletes who 'are pressed, racked, worn out.'[100] Athletes can submit themselves for ten months to strenuous exercises and strict discipline, completely forbidding themselves from the life of ease and luxury, all in the hope of winning a race that will last a mere few minutes or an hour at most, and obtaining nothing more than a garland of flowers as a reward.

Then should not Christians willingly submit themselves to the demands of the life of holiness, giving up the ego and forsaking pleasure, in order to present their bodies as a living sacrifice, holy and acceptable to God (cf. Rom. 12:1)?

The time an athlete spends in training is viewed as time set apart for his own good. It is a time in which he gives up certain things which, while not evil in themselves, would hinder him from achieving his goal.

In the same way, when a Christian gives up the things of this life and its pleasures, it is not because he considers those things sinful or forbidden, but because they are obstacles standing between him and the service entrusted to him.

If a believer would only place the example of the athlete before his eyes and try to strive like him in forsaking and keeping away from pleasures, what a holy, powerful and God-glorifying life he would lead!

---

[100] Tertullian, *To the Martyrs*, 3 (ANF 3:694).

SPIRITUAL UNDERSTANDING OF PHYSICAL TRAINING

A Crown that Perishes and a Crown that Does not

The best an athlete can hope to achieve is victory in the race and attaining the crown. The crown—*stéphanos*[101]—was a garland of flowers placed one the victor's head, which would not remain in bloom for more than a few days. It was for this perishing crown that an athlete would struggle and persevere and discipline himself in everything. But the crown the Christian strives for is a crown that endures forever; a crown placed upon sweat and struggle of their entire lifetime: 'Be faithful until death, and I will give you the crown of life' (Rev 2:10).

'I Run Thus; not With Uncertainty'

This means that I run the course of the race always keeping before my eyes the goal for which I am striving. To run with 'uncertainty'—*adílōs*—would be to run without having the goal clearly before one's eyes, without a definite goal in one's heart and mind.[102] Many run the race and many struggle, even to the point of giving their body up to be burned (cf. 1 Cor. 13:3), but when the reason for running is unclear, or when the goal is unworthy of the degree of labour and hardship endured for its sake, the struggler will soon abandon his course

---

[101] The first person to attain the crown of martyrdom in the early Church was Stephen the Archdeacon, whose name means 'a crown'.
[102] Cf. *GELNT*: 16.

and surrender his weapons while he is still halfway along the track.

One of the most beautiful contemplations on this theme, showing how a competitor without a goal before his eyes will quickly be overcome by despair and give up, is from St Hilarion, father of Palestinian monasticism:

> Consider the hunting dogs which chase after hares; imagine one of these dogs sees a hare in the distance and immediately gives chase; the other dogs that are with him see this dog taking off and take off after him, even though they have not seen the hare. They will continue running with him, but only for a time; when at length the effort and struggle exhaust them, they give up the chase and turn back. However the dog that saw the hare continues chasing it by himself. He does not allow the effort or the struggle to hinder him from completing his long course. He risks his life as he goes on, giving himself no rest. He does not allow the turning aside of the other dogs behind him to put him off. He goes on running until he has caught the hare he saw. He is careless both of the stumbling blocks in his path, whether stones or thorns, and of the wounds they have inflicted on him.

> So also the brother who wishes to follow after the love of Christ must fix his gaze upon the Cross until he catches up with Him that was crucified upon it, even though he sees everyone else has begun to turn back.[103]

---

[103] E. A. W. Budge (ed.), *Paradise of the Holy Fathers* 2.212 (London: Chatto & Windus, 1907): 199. TN: The saying is included in the anonymous collection (N203) and it is also considered

SPIRITUAL UNDERSTANDING OF PHYSICAL TRAINING

In his epistle to the Philippians, St Paul attests to the importance of a competitor keeping his eyes firmly on the goal. One should never turn around to look at the other competitors, to see their successes or their failures. Nor should one look behind him to take stock of how far he has already come. It is the same with one who is striving to completely forget his past and all its missteps and stumblings, always keeping before his eyes the goal and the end for which he is striving: 'forgetting those things which are behind and reaching forward to those things which are ahead, I press toward the goal for the prize of the upward call of God in Christ Jesus' (Phil. 3:13–14).

In the epistle to the Hebrews, St Paul paints a picture of a competitor running in a race while thousands around him encourage and support him. Even so, he must not turn his gaze or concern himself with all the applause and acclaim, but rather look towards the aim for which he runs. A struggler must always keep the Lord Jesus before his eyes as the only goal and end of his struggle. He must free himself from all burdens that hold him back and slow the swiftness of his surging forward, holding fast to such patience as will let him bear the hardships of the path and violence of the race:

Therefore we also, since we are surrounded by so great a

---

anonymous by the Greek systematic collection that attributes it to 'an elder'. The Syriac Collection 'The Paradise of the Fathers' explicitly attributes the saying to St Hilarion. It is from this version that we have taken the text.

ANBA EPIPHANIUS

cloud of witnesses, let us lay aside every weight, and the sin which so easily ensnares us, and let us run with endurance the race that is set before us, looking unto Jesus, the author and finisher of our faith (Heb. 12:1–2).

'I Fight, not as One Who Beats the Air'

The word 'fight' here means 'to box' or strike with the fist. The apostle is speaking here of a boxer who aims his punches at the air without striking his adversary, rendering all his efforts useless. The apostle, in his struggle, does not compare himself with this boxer, for unlike this boxer in his combat against evil, he aims his punches so as to hit his target. One might suppose that so long as he is running the race with the other runners, so long as he is dealing punches, even though they only strike the air, he will still be crowned. But the Apostle says openly, 'If anyone competes in athletics, he is not crowned unless he competes according to the rules' (2 Tim. 2:5). Our struggle does not depend on the strength of our muscles or heroic feats of the body; rather, it fundamentally depends on God who works within us and supports us, 'for it is God who works in you both to will and to do for His good pleasure' (Phil. 2:13).

'I Discipline my Body and Bring it into Subjection'

Imagine a boxer in the ring, directing his punches at the face of his opponent, and as a result of the violent blows to the face, his face is painted with bruises, especially beneath the eyes. This is the meaning of the verb *hypōpiázō*, translated here as 'discipline'.[104] We see here that the Apostle Paul does not say that in his struggle his enemy gives him bruises so that he comes away black and blue from the fight. Rather, he resolves to subdue his body and forces it to submit to his will, not waiting for someone else to command him: 'I have learned both to be full and to be hungry, both to abound and to suffer need' (Phil. 4:12). In this he is following in the footsteps of his Master, the Lord Jesus, of Whom it was said, 'For the joy that was set before Him [*that is, of His own will, not the will of others*] endured the Cross, despising the shame, and [*as a result*] has sat down at the right hand of the throne of God' (Heb. 12:2). Disciplining the body does not mean weakening or killing it. One of the saints said, 'We have not been taught to kill our bodies, but to kill our passions.'[105] What is meant here is clarified by the Apostle Paul in his letter to the Colossians: 'Therefore put to death your members which are on the earth: fornication, uncleanness, passion, evil desire, and covetousness, which is idolatry' (Col. 3:5).

'Lest I Myself Should Become Disqualified'

Finally, I fear that after I have trained others and taught them the art of athletic competition and the means of obtaining the crown, I should discover that I am still not fit or qualified to enter the final race. This is what is meant by the word *adókimos*, translated here as

---

[104] Cf. K. Weiss, 'ὑποπιάζω', *TDNT*, VIII: 590–1.
[105] *Sayings of the Desert Fathers*, Poemen 184 (*Ward*: 193).

'disqualified'. This word is used in sporting contexts to mean 'not eligible', because a competitor has broken the rules of training and is not eligible to enter the competition for the crown.[106]

The Apostle Paul sets before us the example of the athlete who separates himself from the pleasures and lusts of the world, renouncing all that is not helpful, forgetting entirely what lies behind him, pushing ahead to what lies before him, not busying himself with the concerns of the world or its hindrances, fastening his gaze on the clearly-defined goal fixed before his eyes: to subject himself to harsh training, because this is what will qualify him to receive the crown. St Paul sums up this whole idea in a piece of advice to his disciple Timothy: 'No one engaged in warfare entangles himself with the affairs of this life, that he may please him who enlisted him as a soldier. And also if anyone competes in athletics, he is not crowned unless he competes according to the rules' (2 Tim. 2:4–5). He exhorts this disciple that if he competes according to the rules, his crown is guaranteed; he must only be ready for the Lord's coming:

> I have fought the good fight, I have finished the race, I have kept the faith. Finally, there is laid up for me the crown of righteousness, which the Lord, the righteous Judge, will give to me on that Day, and not to me only but also to all who have loved His appearing (2 Tim. 4:7–8).

---

[106] Cf. K. S. Wuest, *Bypaths in the Greek New Testament* (Grand Rapids, MI: Eerdmans, 1973): 57.

TRIALS AS THE EXPRESSION OF GOD'S LOVE

The Apostle Paul went about preaching the name of Christ to the east and to the west. He witnessed to Christ before kings, rulers, philosophers, the Jewish high priests, and in the synagogues of the Jews, bringing about the salvation of many. He was caught up to the third heaven in which he heard inexpressible words which it is not lawful for a man to utter (cf. 2 Cor. 12:4). He was granted the gift of casting out demons and of healing sicknesses, even of raising the dead. Yet in spite of this, he was given 'a thorn in the flesh', which he asked God three times to take away, and in which the Lord did not comply.

Why are Christians allowed to experience suffering? Why do they go through the chastening of the Lord? In his epistle to the Hebrews, we hear how the faithful endured reproaches, persecution, imprisonment and dispossession, all on account of their faith. The epistle states that they experienced all these sufferings after they had been enlightened by baptism:

> But recall the former days in which, after you were illuminated, you endured a great struggle with sufferings: partly while you were made a spectacle both by reproaches and tribulations, and partly while you became companions of those who were so treated; for you had compassion on

me in my chains, and joyfully accepted the plundering of your goods (Heb. 10:32–4).

These tribulations almost caused them to lose confidence in the faith, wherefore the Apostle urged them to hold fast to their confidence in God:

> Therefore do not cast away your confidence, which has great reward. For you have need of endurance, so that after you have done the will of God, you may receive the promise (Heb. 10:35–36).

Christians sometimes wonder what is the lesson God wants to teach us through these sufferings. When a Christian comes to understand the divine intention behind trials, they will become capable of patience and of enduring suffering. In the epistle to Hebrews, the Apostle describes sufferings as the chastening of God: 'For whom the Lord loves He chastens, and scourges every son whom He receives' (Heb. 12:6; Prov. 3:12).

How are trials and sufferings a sign of God and the evidence that we have become His children? To answer these questions, we must first know what is intended by the word 'chasten'; then, we will be able to understand God's purpose in chastening and its ultimate end for us.

The word 'chasten' is a translation of the Greek word *paideúō*. This word has two fundamental definitions, each one complimenting the other. The first definition is to rear, train or teach. The second meaning is to

TRIALS AS THE EXPRESSION OF GOD'S LOVE

discipline or punish, referring to the process of disciplining and correcting experienced by a child.[107]

The noun 'chastening' (Heb. 12:7, 8, 11) is a translation of the word *paideía*, which combines both meanings of the previous verb. It refers to the purpose of education in the Greek world, and the process of bringing up and forming a person. In the Acts of the Apostles, it is used in reference to Moses: 'And Moses was learned [*epaideúthē*] in all the wisdom of the Egyptians, and was mighty in words and deeds' (Acts 7:22).

In the Old Testament, there are two Hebrew words that refer to education or training through discipline and correction. They are *yāsar*, which means to discipline or correct, and *mûsār* which means discipline, correction or teaching.[108]

When the Lord established His covenant with Israel in ancient times, He used to discipline the people with love in order to draw them to Himself. Thus, we hear Jeremiah the Prophet declaring: '"For I am with you," says the Lord, "to save you; though I make a full end of all nations where I have scattered you, yet I will not make a complete end of you. But I will correct you in justice, and will not let you go altogether unpunished"' (Jer. 30:11).

His relationship with His people reveals the image of a loving father: 'I will be his Father, and he shall be My son. If he commits iniquity, I will chasten him with the

---

[107] Cf. *TDNT*, V: 608–12.
[108] Cf. *TDNT*, VI 6: 127–34.

rod of men [*i.e. by means of human beings*] and with the blows of the sons of men [*i.e. with the sufferings that human beings bear*]. But My mercy shall not depart from him' (2 Sam. 7:14–15).

The words *yāsar* and *mûsār* are never used to describe the punishment of animals or beasts, or the punishments God visits on the heathen nations. They are rather used to describe God's chastening of His people. Thus, Moses the Prophet says to the people of Israel: 'As a man chastens his son, so the Lord your God chastens you' (Deut. 8:5). Likewise, Solomon the Wise says, 'My son, do not despise the chastening of the Lord, nor detest His correction; for whom the Lord loves He corrects, just as a father the son in whom he delights' (Prov. 3:11–12). And David the Prophet says, 'The Lord has chastened me severely, but He has not given me over to death' (Ps. 118:18).

When the Old Testament was translated into Greek in the translation known as the Septuagint, the words *yāsar* and *mûsār* were translated in most cases with the verb *paideúō*.[109] The translators always had in mind God's relationship with and love for His children as a disciplining father, rather than turning to the concept of discipline and correction according to the principles of childrearing in the Greek world.

---

[109] Cf. P. R. Gilchrist, יסר, in Robert Laird Harris et al. (eds.) *Theological Wordbook of the Old Testament*, I, (Chicago, IL: Moody Press, 1980): 386-387.

TRIALS AS THE EXPRESSION OF GOD'S LOVE

The love that God demonstrates in correcting and disciplining His children is entirely different—sometimes, even contradictory—to the ancient world's approach to raising and correcting children. In the first century AD, a child had no rights with regards to education or upbringing, not even the right to live. In Greco-Roman society, parents had the right to abandon their children, and were under no obligation to pay for their children's living costs or to educate them. It was possible for children in the ancient world to receive education (*paideía*), but this education was not an expression of their parents' love.

However, in the Christian (or Jewish) world, a child was instructed and subjected to chastening to help them on their path to salvation. Timothy received his education from his youth and was instructed in the principles of Holy Scripture, for the word of God is 'profitable for doctrine, for reproof, for correction, for instruction in righteousness' (2 Tim. 3:15–17).

God's will is to turn the hearts of the fathers to their children (cf. Mal. 4:6) and to teach the children the commandments of God (cf. Deut. 6:7). St Paul commanded fathers to bring up their children 'in the training and admonition of the Lord' (Eph. 4:6). A father, therefore, expresses his love for his child by disciplining and instructing him, even if he is sometimes forced to use chastening.

In the same way, God's chastening reveals that we have a heavenly Father who loves us and always watches over us to instruct and correct us. The author of the epistle to the Hebrews had God's love for His children in mind when he quoted the passage: 'whom the Lord loves He chastens', to explain the reason God chastens His children. Here, chastening is the clearest expression of God's fatherly love for us. If we respect our fathers in the flesh when they discipline us, how much more in the case of our Heavenly Father:

> If you endure chastening, God deals with you as with sons; for what son is there whom a father does not chasten?... We have had human fathers who corrected us, and we paid them respect. Shall we not much more readily be in subjection to the Father of spirits and live?' (Heb. 12:7, 9).

Examining Hebrews 12:5–11, we find that the verb 'to chasten' (*paideúō*) is repeated eight times. These verses clearly explain what God's intention is in His chastening. The author of the epistle could have chosen other words with harsher connotations of discipline and punishment such as the verb *kolázō*, for example, which also refers to discipline for the sake of correction, but is not entirely consistent with the goal of bringing up and educating. It is the verb used in the Acts of the Apostles during the trial of the Apostles Peter and John before the chief priests: 'when they had further threatened them, they let them go, finding *no way of punishing* [*kolásōntai*] *them*, because of the people...' (Acts 4:21).

There is also the verb *timōréō* which refers to punishment for the sake of vengeance. It conveys a sense of a victim inflicting a just punishment: 'Of how much worse *punishment* [*timōrías*], do you suppose, will he be thought worthy who has trampled the Son of God underfoot, counted the blood of the covenant by which he was sanctified a common thing, and insulted the Spirit of grace?' (Heb. 10:29).

The verb *dichotoméō* means to inflict the harshest punishment. Its literal meaning is to cut the perpetrator into pieces: 'the master of that servant will come on a day when he is not looking for him and at an hour that he is not aware of, and will *cut him in two* [*dichotomḗsei*] and appoint him his portion with the hypocrites' (Matt .24:50–1).

The verb *ekdikéō* means to punish for the purpose of revenge: 'Beloved, do not *avenge* [*ekdikoúntes*] yourselves' (Rom. 12:19). The verb *zēmióō* means to inflict a punishment that will lead to loss: 'If anyone's work is burned, he will *suffer loss* [*zēmiōthḗsetai*]; but he himself will be saved, yet so as through fire' (1 Cor. 3:15). And the verb *basanizō* means to punish by means of torture and physical suffering (cf. Matt. 8:29).

In ancient literature, these words could describe divine punishment and human punishment alike. Most of the time, criminals were punished with beatings, fines, forced labour in mines, or other various physical torments. Slaves were punished in whatever way their masters pleased. However, the author of Hebrews chooses none of these words to describe the mystery of suffering in the Christian life. Instead, he provides a vivid image of God chastening His children for their spiritual progress. The divine intent to chasten is built upon the foundation of fatherly love.

What then is the purpose of sufferings for the Christian? The Bible describes chastening as painful and grievous (cf. Heb. 12:11), and this is a reality we cannot ignore. But we must not forget that at trying times, God's love is revealed to us that we may come to know Him more closely. God especially chastens us so that 'we may be partakers of His holiness' (Heb. 12:10). He also wants us to learn by experience how to reap peace and righteousness from chastening (cf. Heb. 12:11). He also strengthens us and makes us firm through chastening, so that He may use us to treat the weaknesses of others: 'Therefore strengthen the hands which hang down, and the feeble knees, and make straight paths for your feet, so that what is lame may not be dislocated, but rather be healed' (Heb. 12:12–13). Or, as the Apostle Paul says, '[God] comforts us in all our tribulation, that we may be able to comfort those who are in any trouble, with the comfort with which we ourselves are comforted…' (2 Cor. 1:4).

These blessings which a believer gains through chastening and sufferings turn pain into a necessity which we ought to endure. Let us put before our eyes the blessings that abound to us through the sufferings that the Lord underwent: 'He was wounded for our transgressions, He was bruised for our iniquities; the chastisement for our peace was upon Him, and by His stripes we are healed' (Isa. 53:5). The Lord Jesus endured the Cross and the insults of sinners for the sake of the joy that was set before Him, and sat down at the right hand of the Majesty on high (cf. Heb. 12:2–3). His sufferings granted us salvation, and therefore, we should not despair or grow weak on account of sufferings (cf. Heb. 12:3).

Indeed, the Apostle Paul struggled and preached the Gospel, attained gifts of teaching of healing and the rest of the gifts of the Holy Spirit. Yet the thorn he had received in his body was greater than all the gifts he had obtained, because it preserved all these gifts for him. St Paul refers to this truth in his own way when he said:

> It is doubtless not profitable for me to boast. I will come to visions and revelations of the Lord... And lest I should be exalted above measure by the abundance of the revelations, a thorn in the flesh was given to me, a messenger of Satan to buffet me, lest I be exalted above measure. Concerning this thing I pleaded with the Lord three times that it might depart from me. And He said to me, "My grace is sufficient for you, for My strength is made perfect in weakness." Therefore most gladly I will rather boast in my infirmities, that the power of Christ may rest upon me. Therefore I take pleasure in infirmities, in reproaches, in needs, in persecutions, in distresses, for Christ's sake. For when I am weak, then I am strong (2 Cor. 12:1, 7–10).

OUR LIFE IN CHRIST

In the Acts of the Apostles, we read:

"Brethren and fathers, hear my *defence [apología]* before you now." And when they heard that he spoke to them in the Hebrew *language [diálektos], they kept all the more silent [hēsychía]*. Then he said: "I am indeed a Jew, born in Tarsus of Cilicia, but brought up in this city at the feet of Gamaliel, taught according to the strictness of our fathers' law, and was zealous toward God as you all are today. I persecuted this Way to the death, binding and delivering into prisons both men and women, as also the high priest bears me witness, and all the council of the elders [*presbytérion*], from whom I also received letters to the brethren, and went to Damascus to bring in chains even those who were there to Jerusalem to be punished. Now it happened, as I journeyed and came near Damascus at about noon, suddenly *a great light from heaven shone around me* [peri*astrápsai fōs ikanón* perí *emé*]. And I fell to the ground and heard a voice saying to me, 'Saul, Saul, why are you persecuting Me?' So I answered, 'Who are You, Lord [*Kýrie*]?' And He said to me, 'I am Jesus of Nazareth, whom you are persecuting.' And those who were with me indeed saw the light and were afraid, but *they did not hear the voice of Him who spoke to me* [*tḗn dé fōnḗn ouk ḗkousan toú laloúntós moi*]. So I said, 'What shall I do, Lord?' And the Lord said to me, 'Arise and go into Damascus, and there you will be told all things which are appointed for you to do.' And since I could not see *for the glory of that* *light* [*tés dóxēs toú fōtós ekeínou*], being led by the hand of those who were with me, I came into Damascus. Then a certain Ananias, a devout man according to the law, having a good testimony with all the Jews who dwelt there, came to me; and he stood and said to me, 'Brother Saul, receive your sight.' And at that same hour I looked up at him. Then he said, '*The God of our fathers* [*ho Theós tōn patérōn ēmōn*] [i.e. God the Father] *has chosen you* [*proecheirísato*][110] that you should know His will, and see *the Just One* [*tón Díkaion*] [i.e. God the Son], and hear the voice of His mouth.[111] For you will be His witness to all men of what you have seen and heard. And now why are you waiting? Arise and be baptized, and wash away your sins, calling on the name of the Lord' (Acts 22:1–16).

We all know the story of how St Paul the Apostle came to faith. After St Stephen had been stoned, while the young Saul of Tarsus guarded the garments of those who were carrying out the stoning, the Book of Acts tells us:

> Now Saul was consenting to his death. At that time a great persecution arose against the church which was at Jerusalem; and they were all scattered throughout the regions of Judea and Samaria, except the apostles. And devout men carried Stephen to his burial, and made great lamentation over him. As for Saul, he made havoc of the church,

---

[110] Cf. Gal 1:15–16, 'But when it pleased God, who separated me from my mother's womb and called me through His grace, to reveal His Son in me, that I might preach Him among the Gentiles, I did not immediately confer with flesh and blood…'

[111] Cf. Acts 9:17, 'that you may… be filled with the Holy Spirit.'

entering every house, and dragging off men and women, committing them to prison (Acts 8:1–3).

After this, the Book of Acts reports:

Then Saul, still breathing threats and murder against the disciples of the Lord, went to the high priest and asked letters from him to the synagogues of Damascus, so that if he found any who were of the Way, whether men or women, he might bring them bound to Jerusalem (Acts 9:1–2).

On the road to Damascus, the Lord appeared to St Paul in this vision. This was the most important and fundamental experience of his life. He never afterward ceased to penetrate more deeply into its meaning and proclaim its content. He began this proclamation with great energy ever since this first spiritual experience on the Damascus road; the profound effect of this event upon him is evident in the way he repeats it on all occasions. In the Acts of the Apostles, the story is repeated three times in full detail (Acts 9:1–9; 22:6–16; 26:12–18).

There are two important expressions that deserve attention in the accounts of this appearance. These two expressions became the beginning of the inspired vision that St Paul drew from the Lord of our being and new existence in Christ, and of the Church which is His body.

One of the most important details in this account is the phrase 'shone around me', which is repeated in all three passages in which the story is related. An analysis of the Greek reveals the force with even greater clarity.[112] The light shone *around him*, immersing the Apostle within. It was not simply a light that appeared before him, but a new, luminous environment that enveloped him.

From the centre of this luminous environment that flooded over him, a voice came to him saying, 'Saul, Saul, why are you persecuting Me?' This is the second important phrase. It is surprising that the Apostle perceived immediately that it was the Lord who was speaking with him: 'Who are You, Lord [*Kýrie*]?' He answered him: 'I am Jesus, whom you are persecuting.' But given that Paul was persecuting men and women, dragging them into prison, how could the Lord say that it was *Him* whom Paul is persecuting? Was it here that Paul perceived the extremely strong connection—a connection at the level of being—between the Lord and those men and women whom he was persecuting? For this meant that those people were one being [or one entity] with Jesus who was speaking to him and Who was the centre of that light.

This was the beginning of his understanding of the mystery of Christ. He learned afterwards that the Lord nourished these people with His Body and Blood. He understood why these people were one being with the Lord: the Lord gave them His body to eat, so those men

---

[112] In Acts 9:3, *periéstrapsen* from *peri*: around and *astrapé*: lightning. In Acts 26:13, *perilámpsan* from *peri*: around and *lámpō*: to shine. Acts 22:6 is even stronger, using *peri* twice: *periastrápsai* ... . *perí emé* (around me).

and women had the Lord's body within them, and therefore, whoever persecuted them was persecuting the Lord Himself by persecuting His body! In this way, he began to perceive the mystery of the divine body, which contains the inexpressible riches of Christ; the mystery of the Church, that is, His body, the fulness that fills all!

From this moment, Paul began to comprehend the reality of Christ and the reality of our existence in Him. The Holy Spirit increased in him understanding and the declaration of the knowledge of this mystery, until this mystery reigned over his entire being and filled his mind and heart, becoming the reigning theme in the writing of all his epistles: *we are in Christ, and Christ is in us*.

When any one of the disciples speaks of this reality, we say that they heard it from the Lord Himself when He was in their midst, revealing to them the mysteries of the kingdom of God. In the same way, St Paul's understanding came to him in a personal declaration from the Lord Jesus.

The Lord Jesus declared this truth to His disciples many times. He mentioned it first with respect to His relationship with God the Father, when the Apostle Phillip asked Christ saying: 'Lord, show us the Father, and it is sufficient for us' (John 14:8).

> Do you not believe that I am in the Father, and the Father in Me? The words that I speak to you I do not speak on My own authority; but the Father who dwells in Me does the works (John 14:10).

He then applies these words to His relationship with us:

> At in that day you will know that I am in My Father, and you in Me, and I in you (John 14:20).

> I in them, and You in Me; that they may be made perfect in one, and that the world may know that You have sent Me, and have loved them as You have loved Me (John 17:23).

> And I have declared to them Your name, and will declare it, that the love with which You loved Me may be in them, and I in them (John 17:26),

The disciples understood these words, and so we find St John reiterating them in his epistles, saying:

> Whoever confesses that Jesus is the Son of God, God abides in him, and he in God. And we have known and believed the love that God has for us. God is love, and he who abides in love abides in God, and God in him (1 John 4:15–16).

> Therefore let that abide in you which you heard from the beginning. If what you heard from the beginning abides in you, you also will abide in the Son and in the Father (1 John 2:24).

> But the anointing which you have received from Him abides in you, and you do not need that anyone teach you; but as the same anointing teaches you concerning all things, and is true, and is not a lie, and just as it has taught you, you will abide in Him (1 John 2:27).

This is what the Lord Jesus revealed to His disciples, and what His disciples and apostles announced to us.

And this is what the Lord Jesus revealed to Paul in the vision on the Damascus road, and which He taught him many times afterwards through various revelations: 'By revelation He made known to me the mystery, as I have briefly written already, by which, when you read, you may understand my knowledge in the mystery of Christ' (Eph. 3:3–4), and, 'For I neither received it from man, nor was I taught it, but it came through the revelation of Jesus Christ' (Gal. 1:12).

What is the mystery that was revealed to St Paul, which he then announced to us? St Paul mentions this mystery several times in his letters to the people of Ephesus and Colossae:

> …having made known to us the mystery of His will, according to His good pleasure which He purposed in Himself, that in the dispensation of the fullness of the times *He might gather together in one all things in Christ*, both which are in heaven and which are on earth—in Him (Eph. 1:9–10).

> …by revelation He made known to me the mystery (as I have briefly written already, by which, when you read, you may understand my knowledge in the mystery of Christ), which in other ages was not made known to the sons of men, as it has now been revealed by the Spirit to His holy apostles and prophets: *that the Gentiles should be fellow heirs, of the same body*, and partakers of His promise in Christ through the Gospel (Eph. 3:3–6).

> …the mystery which has been hidden from ages and from generations, but now has been revealed to His saints. To them God willed to make known what are the riches of

the glory of this mystery among the Gentiles: which is Christ in you, the hope of glory (Col 1:26–7).

It is clear that St Paul—when he was surrounded by the light from all sides—sensed what it meant to be within the Divine Light, and so understood the meaning of the words: 'Why are you persecuting Me?' Any honour or insult that befalls Christians falls upon Christ personally. St Paul mentioned this in his epistle to the Ephesians:

> For we are members of His body, of His flesh and of His bones. "For this reason a man shall leave his father and mother and be joined to his wife, and the two shall become one flesh." This is a great mystery, but I speak concerning Christ and the church (Eph 5:30–32).

This mystery has great theological significance in Christian thought, but it also has a *moral significance* that governs a Christian's life and conduct throughout his or her life. In Christianity, moral values do not spring from educational or social principles, but from the notion of our communion and unity in the body of Christ. Listen to what the Apostle Paul says:

> Children, obey your parents *in* the Lord, for this is right (Eph. 6:1).

Here, obedience is *in the Lord*; not simply for the sake of the Lord, or to please the Lord, or from fear of the Lord. What does it mean for children to obey their parents '*in* the Lord'? It means to obey them considering that they and their parents are members of the one body of the Lord. So just as the members submit to one

OUR LIFE IN CHRIST

another in perfect harmony for the good of the whole body, so also children ought to submit to their parents for the good of the body of Christ and out of love for that body's master.

In his epistle to the Colossians, St Paul applies this notion to the relationship between a wife and her husband:

> Wives, submit to your own husbands, as is fitting *in* the Lord (Col. 3:18).

In fact, we can go even further and say that even when the phrase 'in the Lord' is not used, all of St Paul's moral teaching is built on the reality of Christ as the new medium in which we live. Thus, when dealing with a particular kind of sin—sins of the body—he speaks on the basis of this truth:

> Do you not know that your bodies are members of Christ? Shall I then take the members of Christ and make them members of a harlot? Certainly not! (1 Cor. 6:15).

Likewise, when dealing with the problem of division and factionalism that afflicted the church of Corinth, he reminds them that they are the body of Christ, and asks them in astonishment: 'Is Christ divided?' (1 Cor. 1:13), that is, is it possible for Christ to have two bodies so that you can have two factions?! Paul was horrified at the spirit of factionalism that was widespread among them because it was a sin that struck at the very heart of the Lord's body!

Hear what St Cyril the Great says about our unity and existence in Christ:

How should we understand that saying which says: 'That they all may be one, as You, Father, are in Me, and I in You; that they also may be one in Us... I in them, and You in Me; that they may be made perfect in one' (John 17:21, 23)? Wanting to offer mankind a great and supernatural grace, the Logos of God attracts everyone to a union with Himself. On the one hand, in fact, having worn the human body, He has entered into us. On the other hand, he has the Father in Himself, as His Logos and His radiance. It is, therefore, as if He were saying: 'I am in them because of the fact that I wear their own body, and You, Father, are in Me because of the fact that I am of Your same substance. Thus, I want them too to mix with a certain unity by joining one another, as if they were one single body, so that all may be in me, as if I carried them all through the only Temple [My body] that I took on. So they will be and they will appear perfect, for I, though I have become a man, am perfect.'[113]

On the one body, St John Chrysostom says:

'The bread which we break, is it not a communion of the Body of Christ? For we, who are many, are one bread, one body' (1 Cor. 10:16-17). "For why speak I of communion?" he says, "we are that self-same body." For what is the bread? The Body of Christ. And what do they become who partake of it? The Body of Christ: not many bodies, but one body. For as the bread consisting of many grains is made one, so that the grains appear nowhere; they exist, but their difference is not seen by reason of their conjunction so are we conjoined both with each other and with

---

[113] Cyril of Alexandria, *Treasury of the Trinity*, 122 (PG75,204c). Translated from the original Greek.

Christ: there not being one body for thee, and another for thy neighbour to be nourished by, but the very same for all. Wherefore he adds, "For we all partake of the one bread." Now if we are all nourished of the same and all become the same, why do we not also show forth the same love, and become also in this respect one? For this was the old way too in the time of our forefathers: "For the multitude of them that believed were of one heart and soul (Acts 4:32).""[114]

---

[114] John Chrysostom, *Homilies on First Corinthians*, 24.4 (*NPNF* 1/12:140). Lightly modernised.

GAIN AND LOSS
IN ST PAUL'S PROFITABLE BUSINESS

In ancient times, Palestine occupied an important geographical position which made it a meeting point of trade routes in the first century AD. Egypt lay at its southern border, and Mesopotamia to the East, making it a major corridor for trade and an important passageway for armies and caravans. During Old Testament times, most business dealings were done in cities, especially at harbour towns and cities that lay on caravan routes.

By the time of New Testament trade routes had developed and commerce between Palestine and the Roman world was more complicated. This was because, since the invasion of Alexander the Great, the harbour cities of the Mediterranean had fallen under the control of the Roman Empire. As a result, these cities rapidly grew and expanded, and were infiltrated by Greek language and culture. These cities began to depend on trade as a fundamental source of income, whereas before they had previously relied mostly on farming.

It was in one of these trade cities—Tarsus, in the south-eastern region of Asia Minor—that St Paul was born. Tarsus was famous as a centre of culture and trade, and provided the Apostle Paul with the opportunity to learn Koine Greek, a language spoken very widely, especially in business contexts.

Paul was a Pharisee, well-educated in Jewish law. He studied in Jerusalem under Gamaliel, a teacher of the law (cf. Acts 5:34). All students of the Law were required to perform some sort of manual work to support themselves, and it was forbidden for teachers of the law to earn a profit from their profession as teachers. Gamaliel himself worked as a maker of tools; as for Paul, he learned the craft of tentmaking (cf. Acts 18:3).

After the Lord Jesus appeared to Paul on the road to Damascus, his life underwent a fundamental transformation. Instead of a tentmaker, Paul became 'a wise master builder' (1 Cor. 3:10), building up souls for the kingdom of God. Just as the Lord Jesus had used analogies and parables from people's lives to explain the mysteries of the Kingdom of Heaven, the Apostle Paul used terms and expressions from the language of commerce and trade to describe his new relationship with Christ.

Thus, in his epistle to the Philippians, he says:

> But what things were gain to me, these I have counted *loss* for Christ. Yet indeed I also count all things *loss* for the excellence of the knowledge of Christ Jesus my Lord, for whom I have suffered the *loss* of all things, and count them as rubbish, that I may *gain* Christ ... (Phil. 3:7–8).

The Greek word for *gain*—*kérdos*—denotes financial gain or profit; it is used nowhere in the New Testament except by the Apostle Paul, and does not appear in the Septuagint at all.

GAIN AND LOSS...

'For to me, to live is Christ, and to die is *gain*' (Phil. 1:21)

For there are many insubordinate ... whose mouths must be stopped, who subvert whole households, teaching things which they ought not, for the sake of dishonest *gain* (Titus 1:10–11).

The verb form of this word—*kerdaínō*—means to make a profit, to gain, or to escape harm, and it is used sixteen times in the New Testament.[115]

The Greek word used for *loss* is *zēmía*, which means 'loss, harm or damage'. Its meaning is opposite to gain. In a financial context, it means a loss of money or property. This word also appears in the New Testament only on the mouth of the Apostle Paul:

Paul advised them, saying, "Men, I perceive that this voyage will end with disaster and much *loss* [*zēmía*], not only of the cargo and ship, but also our lives" (Acts 27:9–10; cf. Acts 27:21).

This word's verb form—*zēmióō*—means to lose, to suffer harm or suffer punishment. It occurs in the New Testament six times.[116]

St Paul Checks His Account

In the epistle to the Philippians (3:5–6), St Paul counts up his achievements and his inheritance. Technically speaking, these are not the sort of thing that can be lost, as one might lose merchandise at sea for example. But St Paul knew that these things that already lost

---

[115] Cf. *GELNT*: 430.
[116] Cf. *GELNT*: 338–9.

their value; that is to say, everything that he once considered costly, precious and valuable lost its value and amounted to nothing next to the greatness of the 'knowledge of Christ'. The Apostle Paul manifested this sense in his conduct and his service. The Lord Jesus had said 'where your treasure is, there your heart will be also' (Matt. 6:21), and so Paul found his precious treasure in 'the knowledge of Christ'. Everything that had value became 'in Christ', not in his achievements and inheritance.

It seems that Paul's opponents (Phil. 3:2) had presented their credentials to the church of Philippi, emphasising their Jewish heritage as evidence of their superiority. To this, Paul responded that if the others had presented an account statement detailing the 'origin of their possessions', he ought also to make a statement of his accounts, and so reveal that he had possessed far more than they. In the credit column of his balance statement, he stated that (Phil. 3:5–6):

[He was] 'circumcised the eighth day': he was a Jew of pure blood, keeping the covenant of Abraham, father of fathers.

'Of the stock of Israel': a member of the community which was granted the promises and covenants and the law.

'Of the tribe of Benjamin': a tribe of good repute, which produced the first king of Israel.

'A Hebrew of the Hebrews': he traced his roots back to Abraham, the first to be called a Hebrew (Gen. 14:13).

GAIN AND LOSS...

'*A Pharisee*': of the community that separated itself for the study and keeping of God's law.

'*Zealous*': to the extent that he persecuted the first church in Jerusalem because by following the teaching of Christ, they had deviated from the teaching of Moses.

'*Concerning the righteousness which is in the law, blameless*': he was, in his own eyes, blameless before the law.

But when he put all these distinctions alongside the greatness of *the knowledge of Christ*, he felt that they amounted to nothing more than rubbish. None of these gains and achievements had the same value in his eyes that they did before. So, he stopped competing for them; he had no desire to invest in them for a greater profit. Instead, he happily crossed them out of his account statement. Paul had discovered that 'one pearl of great price, went and sold all that he had and bought it' (Matt. 13:46).

People try to put their money in banks and investment companies in the form of shares or bonds. But when the shares drop in value, so does their profit. The shareholder does not lose the shares themselves when they lose their value—he still owns them—but, he no longer values them as he did.

In the same way, Paul still possessed his Jewish credentials, but he now saw them as a bad investment compared to the precious pearl of great price he had obtained. Let us run through Paul's former shares, but this time, from the perspective of our own day: he came from a prestigious family of good reputation; he had attained the highest university qualifications; he was proficient in a number of foreign languages; he had a prominent place in society and was on the international stage. He was—in his own eyes and in the eyes of all—a man of righteousness, godliness and illustrious deeds.

But, when he compared this inheritance and these gains to the knowledge of Christ, he found that all of them amounted to rubbish, having no worth to him at all. The value of his qualifications being thus diminished, he had to start trading in a different field that might prove more profitable, and that field was the knowledge of Christ. What is meant here is not intellectual knowledge of Christ, of the sort he might get from books and lectures, but experiential knowledge of Christ that comes from long intimacy with God and conversation with Him; the sort of knowledge that made Paul cry out, 'that I may know Him and the power of His Resurrection, and the fellowship of His sufferings, being conformed to His Death, if, by any means, I may attain to the resurrection from the dead' (Phil. 3:10–11).

He placed his entire former life on the scales, and finding that it weighed nothing, he counted it as rubbish. He then placed the knowledge of Christ on the other side of the balance, and found it equal to eternal life: 'And *this is eternal life, that they may know You*, the only true God, and Jesus Christ whom You have sent' (John 17:3). Thus, Paul was very wise indeed to say, 'I determined not to know anything among you except Jesus Christ and Him crucified' (1 Cor. 2:2).

GAIN AND LOSS...

The Lord Jesus prayed that his disciples would know God, and here again the intention is not intellectual knowledge, but that living knowledge in which the Lord Jesus comes to dwell in the heart: 'And I have declared to them Your name, and will declare it, that the love with which You loved Me may be in them, and *I in them*'" (John 17:26).

There is an important measure by which we can tell whether or not we have known God with true knowledge or merely intellectual knowledge. The measure is summed up by St John the Apostle in a single word: love; love of God and love of one's neighbour:

> Beloved, let us love one another, for love is of God; and everyone who loves is born of God *and knows God*. He who does not love does not know God, for God is love' (1 John 4:7–8).

> Now by this we know that we know Him, if we keep His commandments. He who says, "I know Him", and does not keep His commandments, is a liar, and the truth is not in him. But whoever keeps His word, truly *the love of God* is perfected in him (1 John 2:3–5).

As a tentmaker, St Paul knew the value of his handiwork and the price at which he needed to sell it in order to make a profit. He also understood that the sources on which he relied for profit were not to last forever. The old sources became worthless, but the new sources of great and stable value were 'the excellence of the knowledge of Christ Jesus my Lord' (Phil. 3:8).

ANBA EPIPHANIUS

St Gregory the Theologian sums all of this up when—speaking of the old sources—he compares them to the knowledge of Christ which leads to heavenly and divine blessings:

What is this new mystery which concerns me?

I am small and great, lowly and exalted, mortal and immortal, earthly and heavenly. I share one condition with the lower world, the other with God; one with the flesh, the other with the spirit. I must be buried with Christ, arise with Christ, Be joint heir with Christ, become the son of God, yea, God Himself!

This is the purpose of the great mystery for us. This is the purpose for us of God, Who for us was made man and became poor, to raise our flesh, and recover His image, and remodel man, that we might all be made one in Christ (Eph. 3:28), Who was perfectly made in all of us all that He Himself is (cf. Col. 3:11), that we might no longer be male and female (cf. Gal. 4:28), Barbarian, Scythian, bond or free, which are badges of the flesh (cf. Col. 3:11),

But might bear in ourselves only the stamp of God, by Whom and for Whom we were made, and have so far received our form and model from Him, that we are recognized by it alone.[117]

Before the knowledge Christ we formerly had many different labels and attributes—free persons and slaves, males and females, Jews and Gentiles, rich and poor, educated and illiterate—but after the knowledge of Christ Jesus our Lord, all these labels have become secondary.

---

[117] Gregory the Theologian, *Oration* 7.23 (*NPNF* 2/7:237).

GAIN AND LOSS...

For we have been united with the source of true riches—we who will become like Him—because we shall see Him as He is (1 John 3:2).

COALS OF FIRE

In St Paul's epistle to the Romans, after having explained the great truths of the faith and the relationship between the law and grace, he wrote—in the twelfth chapter—some important pieces of advice for Christians to live by. He also explained the concept of love and peace in Christianity. However, in verse 20 of this chapter (specifically, in the second half of this verse), he provides a quotation from the Book of Proverbs (Prov. 25:22) that has confused many of those who have tried to interpret it, because it seems to contradict the teaching of St Paul the Apostle—and Christianity in general—that commands us to love our enemies. The Apostle Paul says:

> Beloved, do not avenge yourselves, but rather give place to wrath; for it is written, "Vengeance is Mine, I will repay," says the Lord. Therefore:
> "If your enemy is hungry, feed him;
> If he is thirsty, give him a drink;
> For in so doing you will heap coals of fire on his head."
> Do not be overcome by evil, but overcome evil with good (Rom. 12:19–21).

Chapter 12 begins with the words, 'I beseech you therefore'; that is, in response to the grace of Christ that Paul discussed in the previous chapters, he is asking them to present their bodies 'a living sacrifice, holy, acceptable to God' (Rom. 12:1). He goes on to explain in the next passage what it means to be a living sacrifice, and what they ought to do to honour the different gifts entrusted to each one of them which, because of their variety, enrich the Church and fashion them all into one body of Christ (Rom. 12:3–8).

In the following passage (vv. 9–13) the Apostle Paul lays the foundation upon which the community ought to be built up in the form of thirteen commandments; commandments which allow the community to live and grow in *love*:

> Let love be without hypocrisy. Abhor what is evil. Cling to what is good. Be kindly affectionate to one another with brotherly love, in honour giving preference to one another; not lagging in diligence, fervent in spirit, serving the Lord; rejoicing in hope, patient in tribulation, continuing steadfastly in prayer; distributing to the needs of the saints, given to hospitality (Rom. 12:9–13).

In the verses that come after this (vv. 14–17), he provides a further set of commandments which, if they are obeyed, will cause the community to live in *peace*, both within itself and towards others:

> Bless those who persecute you; bless and do not curse. Rejoice with those who rejoice, and weep with those who weep. Be of the same mind toward one another. Do not set your mind on high things, but associate with the humble. Do not be wise in your own opinion. Repay no one evil for evil. Have regard for good things in the sight of all men (Rom. 12:14–17).

He then sums all this up (v. 18) with a commandment to bring about peace in the entire community: 'If it is possible, as much as depends on you, live peaceably with all men' (Rom. 12:18).

The driving concern in the epistle to the Romans that runs through all the verses, especially verses 19–21, and which, if ignored, will lead to division and disorder in the Church in Rome, is the example of Christ that appears clearly in Romans 5:10: 'For if when we were enemies we were reconciled to God through the Death of His Son.' It is not that we were righteous or holy, and so became worthy for Christ to die for our sake; rather, we were enemies, disobedient and rebellious, and all of us destitute of the glory of God. But even so, Christ died for our sake. What then, should be our attitude to our enemies, after we have been reconciled to God?

The epistle to the Romans proceeds to offer advice that will encourage the community to live together in unity and harmony. Thus, in chapter 13, he urges them to live in peace with the civil authorities, and in chapters 14 and 15, he curbs the growing tension between Jews and Gentiles about types of food and concepts of purity and impurity, before closing the epistle with a greeting for all the members of the church who were living together in peace and love.

Turning back now to Romans 12:19–21, and what the Apostle Paul says there about peace in the community—'Beloved, do not avenge yourselves… Do not be overcome by evil, but overcome evil with good'— we should not be surprised at these verses, for they are the necessary consequence that follows from all that Paul had taught throughout the entire epistle. But these verses are also a clear echo of the Lord Jesus' Sermon on the Mount: 'But I say to you, love your enemies, bless those who curse you, do good to those who hate you' (Matt. 5:44). This is the measure by which we can tell whether the church, or any church, is a living church that follows the teachings of the Lord Jesus and pure Apostles, or whether it is a church according to the verse, 'But if you bite and devour one another, beware lest you be consumed by one another!' (Gal. 5:15).

We come now to verse 20:

Therefore: "If your enemy is hungry, feed him; if he is thirsty, give him a drink; *for in so doing you will heap coals of fire on his head*" (Rom. 12:20).

The first half of this verse agrees perfectly well with the rest of Paul's teachings in this epistle, but the second half comes as a shock and a stumbling block to many. Does heaping coals of fire on the head of an enemy represent some kind of love or mercy toward him?

At first glance, the answer seems to be no: this is a sort of vengeance against the enemy, whereas the first half of the verse accords with the Parable of the Last Judgement in which the Lord Jesus commands us to be merciful to all, whom He calls "the least of these My brethren" (Matt. 25:40).

The early Church resisted interpretations of this verse as endorsing personal vengeance against an enemy in two ways. The first appears in the writings of several Church Fathers such as St John Chrysostom, who interprets the verse to mean that if we do good to my enemy and he still persists in his animosity, this persistence will render him liable in the end to divine judgement; it is as though we were confirming the judgement of God on the Last Day.

There is a hint of the notion of heaping coal's on an enemy's head in the Book of Esdras, a book of the Jewish Apocrypha: 'Let no sinner say that he has not sinned; for God will burn coals of fire on the head of him who says, "I have not sinned before God and his glory"' (2 Esdras 16:53 [RSV]). There is a figurative expression in the Psalms that carries the same meaning: 'Let burning coals fall upon them; let them be cast into the fire, into deep pits, that they rise not up again' (Ps. 140:10).

Several things about the context of this passage in Romans confirm this interpretation. In the first verse of the passage, the Apostle Paul entreats the believers not to avenge themselves, but to leave vengeance up to the judgement of God (Rom. 12:19). You must do good to your enemy and leave it to God to judge him.

The problem with this interpretation is that it is not entirely consistent with the concept of loving one's enemies. I do not do good to my enemy only so that I can bring the wrath of God down upon his head, nor do I offer help to one who hates me so that I can become a cause of condemnation to him.

The second way of interpreting this passage is found in Origen, Augustine, Jerome and Pelagius. In their view, the burning coals of fire on the head of your enemy refers to the shame and disgrace that befall your enemy when you do good to them. Responding to insults with kindness will necessarily lead the enemy to reconsider their stance, which will in turn lead them to repentance. The same explanation can be found in the teachings of the Jewish Rabbis on Proverbs 25:21–22, the verses that Paul quotes in Romans: 'If your enemy is hungry, give him bread to eat; and if he is thirsty, give him water to drink; for so you will heap coals of fire on his head, and the Lord will reward you.' The importance of this interpretation is that it fits with the context of the epistle, and does not conflict with the general Christian concept of love for one's enemies.

At the beginning of the twentieth century, as a result of archaeological investigations concerning the Holy Bible, some light was shed on these verses from Romans and Proverbs. Some scholars have suggested that Proverbs 25:21–22 reflects some features of life in ancient Egypt. The subsequent verse—'The north wind brings forth rain' (Prov. 25:23)—applies to the weather of Egypt, but not that of Palestine.

It was a common practice in ancient Egypt, when one person wronged another, for the offender to put fiery coals in an earthen vessel, carry this vessel on his head and go to the person he had wronged. Here, the fiery coals are not an expression of shame and disgrace *leading to* repentance, as in the interpretation of Origen and Augustine, but a symbol of repentance itself.

The Egyptologist Siegfried Morenz[118] published a report about this ancient Egyptian custom, and scholars have also discovered earthenware jars that were used to carry coals of fire upon the head.[119] According to these investigations, these verses suggest that by doing good to your enemy and so leading him to repentance, he will express this repentance by carrying coals of fire on his head, as a sign that the enmity has ended and a new life of friendship and love begun.

Regardless of the literal interpretation of this verse, we know that every commandment in the Holy Scripture bears with it the power to carry it out. Our fathers experienced the power of these verses and so did good to all who asked them, even if they came with a spirit of antagonism. They all experience the power of change that comes from doing good to others—hundreds of times more powerful than attempts to convince or argue, or to defend oneself even by lawful means.

The *Bustān al-Ruhbān* tells a tale about a struggling monk who was met by thieves who said to him, 'We have come to take everything in your cell.' He replied, 'Take whatever you want, my children!'. They took whatever they could find and left, but forgot a bag

---

[118] Cf. Siegfried Morenz, "Feurige Kohlen auf dem Haupt", in *Theologische Literaturzeitung*, LXXVIII (1953), columns 187–192.

[119] Cf. William Klassen, "Coals of Fire: Sign of Repentance or Revenge?", *New Testament Studies* 9 (1962): 341.

woven from palm leaves. When the old man saw it, he grabbed it and ran after them while shouting: 'My children, take what you have forgotten!' When they saw this, they marvelled at his gentleness and the purity of his heart, and, restoring everything they had taken from his cell, they said to one another, 'Truly, this is a man of God.' This became a cause for repentance, and they both left behind their former life of thievery.[120]

The *Bustān al-Ruhbān* also tells this tale:

> It was said of Abba John the Persian that when some evildoers came to him, he took a basin and wanted to wash their feet. But they were filled with confusion, and began to do penance.[121]

Offer your enemy a cup of cold water. Show him true Christian love rather than trying to discuss his animosity and prove him wrong. The One who gave you the commandment is also able to give you the blessing of obeying it. If your enemy is hungry, feed him bread, and if he is thirsty give him water, for if you do this, you will lead him to repentance and so gain your brother whom the Gospel commanded you to love, even if he is a stranger to your race. As Fr. Matthew the Poor says in his *Commentary on Romans*:

> I feed all who hunger in the person of Christ as though they were Christ, and I give water to all who thirst in the person of Christ as though they were Christ, for I bear the

---

[120] *Apophthegm* 709, in Bustān: 285. Cf. *Sayings of the Desert Fathers*, Euprepius 2 (*Ward*: 62).

[121] *Sayings of the Desert Fathers*, John the Persian 3 (*Ward*: 108)

Spirit of Christ and His gracious love with which He loved me when I was an enemy to Him. A Christian person must announce the Spirit of Christ that is within them. To my enemy, I reveal the Spirit of Christ that is in me through my love and my feeding him and giving him to drink; to this extent, I preach, and all my hope is that my enemy will sense the Spirit of Christ that is in me.[122]

---

[122] Mattā al-Miskīn, *Šarḥ Risālat al-Qiddīs Būlus al-Rasūl ilā Ahl Rūmiyya* (Wādī al-Naṭrūn: Monastery of St Macarius): 574–5.

CHRIST'S TRIUMPHAL PROCESSION

In St Paul's letter to the Colossians, the apostle gives thanks to God the Father, 'who has qualified us to be partakers of the inheritance of the saints in the light. He has delivered us from the power of darkness and conveyed us into the kingdom of the Son of His love' (Col. 1:12–13). He goes on to explain that, if God has delivered us from the power of darkness and set us free from captivity to the enemy, we ought to beware lest anyone try to lead us back into slavery through philosophical sayings, empty deceit and fine words that seem reasonable, and thus fall back into the thrall of the world rather than to Christ (cf. Col. 2:8). For before Christ's coming, we were dead in sins, but through His Resurrection from the dead He made us alive with Him and forgave us all sins (cf. Col. 2:31). By His Resurrection from the dead, Christ triumphed over death and over the devil who had the power of death.[123]

To persuade the Colossians of Christ's victory over death despite all the tribulations they were facing, he describes for them the battle in which Christ vanquished the enemies against whom He fought, and the field on which He was victorious. He then describes the victory

---

[123] TN: Cf. Heb 2:14: '… that through death He might destroy him who had the power of death, that is, the devil'

procession which He led up into heaven: 'Having disarmed principalities and powers, He made a public spectacle of them, triumphing over [*thriambeúsas*] them in it [in the Cross]' (Col. 2:15). Where did St Paul get this image?

A Historical Interlude

The Greek word used by St Paul to describe the victory procession is the verb *thriambeúō*, from which comes the noun *thríambos*. These words entered Latin as *triumphus* and from there into European languages as *triumph*.[124]

In classical Greek literature, this word is used for the ceremonial processions conducted during the feasts of the god Dionysius, the god of vineyards, also known by the name of Bacchus; the processions would move through the city and at the temple dedicated to this god.

Later, the word came to refer to the victory processions led by Roman leaders upon their return from military conflicts. When a Roman leader defeated his enemies, he would return to Rome with a spectacular procession bearing the spoils he had taken from the enemy, and dragging behind him the prisoners he had enslaved. When the procession drew near to Rome, all the people would come out to greet it as it passed through the gates of Rome and advanced through the streets. The commander of the army would lead the procession in a war chariot led by two horses, dressed in a purple

---

[124] Cf. G. Delling, 'θριαμβεύω', *TDNT*, III: 159–60.

CHRIST'S TRIUMPHAL PROCESSION

robe adorned with gold, a crown of victory upon his head, a branch in his right hand and a sceptre in his left tipped with the figure of an eagle. Behind him came the soldiers displaying the spoils of war, waving about in the joy of their victory the gold, silver, pearls and precious gems they won. Next came those Romans who had been liberated from their former captivity, followed by the prisoners captured from the enemy army, bound in shackles. This ceremonial spectacle was capped off at the tail end by teams of musicians, singers and dancers, and finally, the crowds of people accompanying the procession.

The Jewish historian Josephus tells of how the citizens of Rome used to adorn the city with garlands of flowers during these celebrations. He also describes the processions led by Roman emperors such as Vespasian, Titus and Domitian. After Emperor Titus laid siege to Jerusalem and sacked the city, he returned to Rome in a ceremonial procession, and his armies bore with them everything they had plundered from the Temple of Jerusalem, including the lampstand of seven lamps and the golden table, along with some of the tablets and scrolls on which the Law and Torah were inscribed.[125]

Among the proudest features on display in Titus' victory procession were several of the most important leaders of the Jewish Rebellion. Among them was a man named Simeon bar Giora who was captured during the

---

[125] Cf. Josephus, *The Jewish War* 7.5.4–5, trans. Robert Traill, II, (Houlston & Stoneman: London, 1851): 226–8.

siege of the city. This Simeon, whom Josephus brands a tyrant, hid many of his friends in an underground cave during the siege in order to save them from the wrath of the Roman army. When they ran out of food and supplies, they went out of the cave dressed in white robes and red cloaks. Simeon's fate, and that of his friends, was to fall into captivity and be led prisoner through Rome as the most prized captives the army had managed to seize. After the army had paraded him before the people of Rome, they led him to the Temple of Jupiter and executed him there. That was the end of this victory procession.[126]

St Paul adapted in all its details the spectacle of Roman victory procession to bring home to the believers' minds the kind of victory Christ had achieved over the spiritual powers of evil. He says to them: 'Having disarmed principalities and powers, He made a public spectacle of them, triumphing over them in it' (Col. 2:15).

'HAVING SPOILED THE PRINCIPALITIES AND POWERS'

Christ's battle was not against His Jewish crucifiers or the Romans who sentenced Him to Crucifixion, but with the spiritual powers of evil, that is, the Devil and his allies. It was these of whom the Apostle Paul said, 'We do not wrestle against flesh and blood, but against principalities, against powers, against the rulers of the darkness of this age, against spiritual hosts of wickedness in the heavenly places' (Eph. 6:12).

---

[126] Cf. Josephus, *The Jewish War* 7.2.1–2, *ibid.*: 217f.

CHRIST'S TRIUMPHAL PROCESSION

The word 'spoil' gives us an image of how the Lord Jesus dealt with these principalities and authorities. This word was used when a leader was stripped of his rank. It was also used in the law courts when a noble person was convicted of treason and stripped of all his badges and marks of honour he had obtained, and deprived of his rank and station.[127] In the same way, when the Lord clashed with these powers upon the Cross, He stripped them of their power and took away the weapons they relied upon. This is just what the Lord said about these powers before He had entered into battle with them:

> When a strong man, fully armed, guards his own palace, his goods are in peace. But when a stronger than he comes upon him and overcomes him, he takes from him all his armour in which he trusted, and divides his spoils (Luke 11:21–22).
>
> 'I saw Satan fall like lightning from heaven' (Luke 10:18).

In his book on the life of St Antony, St Athanasius says that the demons 'are cowards, and they are utterly terrified by the sign of the Lord's Cross, because in it the Saviour, stripping their armour, made an example of them.'[128]

With the Cross then, the dominion of these powers over creation came to an end. They were made subject to the Son not through willing obedience, but forcibly,

---

[127] Cf. Peter T. O'Brien, *Word Biblical Commentary: Colossians–Philemon*, 44 (Thomas Nelson, 1982): 127.

[128] Athanasius of Alexandria, *Life of Antony* 35, trans. Robert C. Gregg (Mahwah, NJ: Paulist Press, 1980): 57.

since they came up against a power they were unable to resist. They were brought into subjection, but not destroyed, for they are still present, fighting against humanity and tempting mankind. But they cannot harm a person who is firmly established in Christ: 'Simon, Simon! Indeed, Satan has asked for you, that he may sift you as wheat. But I have prayed for you, that your faith should not fail; and when you have returned to Me, strengthen your brethren' (Luke 22:31–2).

St Athanasius explains the role of the Cross in the defeat of Satan and all his works as follows:

> By the sign of the Cross all magic ceases, all witchcraft is brought to naught, all idols are deserted and abandoned, all irrational desire ceases, yet everyone is looking up from earth to heaven![129]

> This He Himself said when He indicated by what manner of death He was going to redeem all, '*When I am lifted up I shall draw all to myself*' (John 12:32)… Yet Christ came that He might overthrow the devil, purify the air, and open up for us the way to heaven, as the Apostle said, '*through the veil, that is, His flesh*' (Heb. 10:20). This must have been by death, and by what other death would these things have happened except that which takes place in the air, I mean, the Cross? For being thus lifted up, He purified the air from the diabolical plots of all demons, saying, '*I saw Satan falling as lightning*' (Luke 10:18), and blazing the

---

[129] Athanasius of Alexandria, *On the Incarnation* 31, trans. John Behr, Greek-English edition (Yonkers, NY: SVS Press, 2011): 117.

CHRIST'S TRIUMPHAL PROCESSION

trail, He made anew the way up to heaven.[130]

'HE MADE A PUBLIC SPECTACLE OF THEM'

This means that He disgraced them openly. The Lord put the principalities and authorities to an open shame, revealing their weakness and impotency, having disarmed them of their weapons and cast them down from their honour and station, and having humiliated them before the entire world.[131] In this way, He gave those who believe in His name the power to rebuke Satan and all his ministers: 'Behold, I give you the authority to trample on serpents and scorpions, and over all the power of the enemy, and nothing shall by any means hurt you' (Luke 10:19); 'Resist the devil and he will flee from you' (James 4:7).

On commenting on the words of the Russian saint John of Kronstadt, Father Matthew the Poor writes:

> The demons are terrified of the sight of the Cross; even the mere sign of it made with the hands. For the Lord Christ triumphed over Satan and all his powers and principalities, stripping them of their authority and openly humiliating them. The sign of the Cross thus became a reminder of their humiliation and a sign of their punishment.[132]

---

[130] *On the Incarnation* 25 (ibid., 105).

[131] Cf. H. Salter, 'δειγματίζω', *TDNT*, II: 31.

[132] Mattā al-Miskīn, *Ḥayāt al-Ṣalāh al-Urṯūḏuksiyya* (Wādī al-Naṭrūn: Monastery of St Macarius, 1986): 572. Cf. John of Kronštadt, *My life in Christ* (London:Cassel & Co., 1897): 253.

ANBA EPIPHANIUS

'Triumphing over Them in It'

The word *triumph* is the focal point of the entire verse; this is the word which relates to triumphal processions. The literal translation would be 'dragged them along in His triumphal procession.' After the Lord had disarmed the principalities, He openly humiliated them before the heavenly powers, leading them along as prisoners in His triumphal procession on the way back to His eternal place at the right hand of the Father.

By using this word, St Paul wanted to paint a picture for us of the battle Christ waged for our sake. He also uses the same word again to illustrate our place in this victory procession:

> Now thanks be to God who always *leads us in triumph* [*thriambeúonti ēmas*] in Christ, and through us diffuses the fragrance of His knowledge in every place (2 Cor. 2:14).

Roman leaders were obliged to hold triumphal processions every time they achieved a victory over their enemies. But the Lord Jesus led His triumphal procession only once, because He had achieved an eternal redemption and sat down at the right hand of the Majesty on high: 'not with the blood of goats and calves, but with His own blood He entered the Most Holy Place once for all, having obtained eternal redemption' (Heb. 9:12).

Roman leaders were accompanied in their processions by Romans who had formerly been captives and had been freed. In the same way, the Lord Jesus leads us in His triumphal procession after He has liberated us from the power of the Devil and delivered us into His kingdom. But we do not march behind Him in His procession; we walk *with* Him and *in* Him: '[He] raised us up together, and made us sit together in the heavenly places in Christ Jesus' (Eph. 2:6).

Roman leaders, in their arrogance and hubris, placed crowns of laurel upon their heads and adorned themselves in royal robes of scarlet as they rode along in their war chariots. As for the humble Lord Jesus, His crown was made of thorns and His chariot was the Cross from atop which He brought about our eternal redemption. His scarlet robe was the blood which stained His body, and flowed out from Him unto the believers.

THE LAST TRUMPET

The inhabitants of Jerusalem used to wake every morning to the sound of a silver trumpet that announced the beginning of a new day. Through the course of the day, trumpets sounded eleven times, proclaiming the offering of the sacrifices and calling the people to worship. The sound of the trumpets was still ringing in the disciples' ears on the day when they asked Lord about the sign of His coming and the end of the age (cf. Matt. 24–25).

When the Lord spoke of the great sound of a trumpet that will accompany His second coming (cf. Matt. 24:31), His words would not have been strange to their ears. The entire people of Israel were eagerly awaiting the sound of heavenly trumpets that would announce the end of this evil world. They looked for the day in which the Lord would punish the wicked heathen nations and reward the righteous people. The fiery proclamation of John the Baptist powerfully awoke this expectation in their hearts, and the preaching of the Lord Jesus and His presence in their midst, persuaded them even further that this end was near. The very air was saturated with hope for the declaration of the end, and the early signs that this hope would come true would be the hearing of the last trumpet.

ANBA EPIPHANIUS

Trumpets in the Old Testament

The Jews of ancient times used two musical instruments, the trumpet and the horn, for calling people to attention. The trumpet (*ḥaṣoṣrâ*) was a straight pipe of silver or brass about two feet long, with a wide, cone-shaped opening on one side and a mouthpiece on the other. It had a sharp, high-pitched sound well-suited to catching attention or frightening enemies.

The horn (*šôfār*) on the other hand, was fashioned from the horns of gazelles or rams. These horns were either left in their natural twisted shape or the curves were straightened out in a furnace. Their sound was dull and harsh, like the harsher wind instruments or the modern car horn.

In the Old Testament, there is a clear distinction between these two instruments, especially in the Hebrew and Aramaic languages in which the Old Testament was written. However, this distinction was lost in the Greek translation of the Old Testament, and consequently, also in the New Testament, where a single word, *sálpinx*, which comes from the verb *salpízō* (to blow the trumpet), is used for both instruments.[1]

Though the horn and the trumpet were different instruments, their function was the same. Both were instruments for calling to attention, used for example, to declare war or call the community together for appointed times of worship. They were not used as musical

---

[1] Cf. Gerhard Friedrich, 'σάλπιγξ,' in *TDNT*, VII: 71-88.

THE LAST TRUMPET

instruments to accompany prayers, songs or anything of that sort. The difference between the two, however, lies in the occasions on which they were used, and by whom they were used. The horn was the favoured instrument of the Levites and soldiers, while the metal trumpet was the instrument of the priests, the children of the High Priest Aaron.

The horn was used to regulate the marching of soldiers, to call people to gatherings, and to warn of danger; it was also used to celebrate the presence the Lord among the gathered. In the Book of Leviticus, God instructed the prophet Moses that the Feast of Atonement should be celebrated as a yearly feast (cf. 23:24), and commanded him saying, 'You shall cause the trumpet (*šôfār/horn*) of the Jubilee to sound on the tenth day of the seventh month; on the Day of Atonement you shall make the trumpet to sound throughout all your land' (Lev. 25:9). He likewise commanded the horn to be used to announce the celebration of the beginning of the year and of the Jubilee, the fiftieth year in which sentences against the people were lifted and in which lands restored to their owners. When the people had surrounded the city of Jericho, it was the sound of a horn that announced the fall of the city's walls (cf. Jos. 6:5, 20), just as it did in the case of the destruction of the Midianites by the people under Gideon's command (cf. Judg. 7:16–18).

Similarly, God commanded Moses to make 'two trumpets of silver' that the priests would use to call the whole congregation together, saying to him, 'The sons of Aaron, the priests, shall blow the trumpets; and these shall be to you as an ordinance forever throughout your generations' (Num. 10:8). The use of metal trumpets thus became restricted to the Temple worship and royal ceremonies. In the Temple of Solomon and in the Second Temple, the sounds of trumpets were heard daily, announcing various occasions for worship such as: the opening of the main gates of the Temple in the morning (three blows of the trumpet) and the offering of the morning and evening sacrifices (nine blows for each offering). The trumpet was also blown when the Psalms were sung, at the beginning of the Sabbath, on the first day of the month, and at the start of the new year.

And so, because of its daily use, the sound the trumpet became a part of the everyday religious customs of the Jews as its sound came to hold spiritual significance. In the Book of Isaiah the Prophet, we read that the sound of trumpets in the Temple will announce the end of the ages and the return of the righteous who are gathered from the ends of the earth:

> 'So it shall be in that day: the great trumpet will be blown; they will come, who are about to perish in the land of Assyria, and they who are outcasts in the land of Egypt, and shall worship the Lord in the holy mount at Jerusalem... And it shall come to pass that from one New Moon to another, and from one Sabbath to another, all flesh shall come to worship before Me,' says the Lord (Isa. 27:13; 66:23).

THE LAST TRUMPET

Instead of announcing the gathering of the people in the Temple, the sound of the trumpet becomes a sign of the return of the people to God through repentance, and of the submission of all peoples to the Lord God and their worshipping before Him. In the time of the Lord Jesus, the Jews associated the sound of the trumpet with the end of the ages, the reappearance of the Messiah, and God's eternal judgement and condemnation of the wicked.

Trumpets in the New Testament

Trumpets are mentioned in the New Testament several times, sometimes simply regarding the ancient Jewish tradition, and sometimes with a symbolic, eschatological meaning.[2] The latter was the meaning at the forefront of the minds of the disciples when they asked the Lord Jesus about the signs of His coming and the end of the ages. Among these mentions [of trumpets in the New Testament] are:

As a Declaration of War: During the Apostle Paul's discussion of the gift of speaking in tongues, he mentions the sound of trumpets as a metaphor to convey the importance of explaining or clarifying the message delivered by those with the gift of tongues, so that their gift will not be useless:

> But now, brethren, if I come to you speaking with tongues, what shall I profit you unless I speak to you either by revelation, by knowledge, by prophesying, or by

---

[2] TN: Eschatological: to do with the end times.

teaching? ... For if the trumpet makes an uncertain sound, who will prepare for battle? (1 Cor. 14:6, 8).

Announcing the Charity of the Rich: During His discourse on the necessity of doing works of mercy in secret, this is mentioned by the Lord Jesus, who severely condemns those who draw attention to their acts of giving. There was a custom during the donation of food and gifts to the poor, in which donations would be announced with the sound of trumpets, in order to encourage the rich to perform the same works of mercy and to ensure that the report of these donations reached the ears of the Lord. But the Lord Jesus commanded alms to be given in secret, without any proclamation or fanfare: 'Therefore, when you do a charitable deed, do not sound a trumpet before you as the hypocrites do in the synagogues and in the streets, that they may have glory from men. Assuredly, I say to you, they have their reward!' (Matt. 6:2).

Announcing the Appearance of God and the Hearing of His Voice: The author of the Epistle to the Hebrews draws a comparison between what the people of ancient times saw on the mountain of Sinai and the glories we have attained in Christ Jesus:

> For you have not come to the mountain that may be touched and that burned with fire, and to blackness and darkness and tempest, and the sound of a trumpet and the voice of words, so that those who heard it begged that the word should not be spoken to them anymore... But you have come to Mount Zion and to the city of the living God, the heavenly Jerusalem, to an innumerable company

of angels, to the general assembly and church of the firstborn who are registered in heaven, to God the Judge of all, to the spirits of just men made perfect, to Jesus the Mediator of the new covenant, and to the blood of sprinkling that speaks better things than that of Abel (Heb 12:18–24).

Darkness, tempest, and the sound of the trumpet accompanied God's appearance. Furthermore, God's own voice is designated as the sound of a trumpet, an indication of clarity and awesomeness at once, just as took place with John the Visionary: 'I was in the Spirit on the Lord's Day, and I heard behind me a loud voice, as of a trumpet, saying, "I am the Alpha and the Omega"' (Rev. 1:10–11); and, 'After these things I looked, and behold, a door standing open in heaven. And the first voice which I heard was like a trumpet speaking with me, saying, "Come up here, and I will show you things which must take place after this"' (Rev. 4:1).

The Eschatological Significance of the Trumpet's Sound: As the sound of the trumpet is used to announce important occasions or as a description of the voice of God when He speaks with human beings, the sound of the trumpet also has a symbolic significance that points to the end times and the entrance into eternity.

Firstly, the sound of the trumpet indicates the general judgement at the end of days. As we have seen in Jewish tradition, an angel at the end of days will blow a great trumpet to gather the lost and exiled from the ends of the earth (cf. Isa. 27:13). The final judgement will not be announced with the sound of just one trumpet, but seven trumpets of angels, an allusion to the fact that the entire world will undergo this judgement. At the sound of the first trumpet, the judgement of God comes forth in the form of natural disasters descending upon all the regions of the world: on the earth, the place inhabited by human beings (cf. Rev. 8:7), on the sea (cf. Rev. 8:8), on the rivers (cf. Rev. 8:10) and on the stars (cf. Rev. 8:12). These disasters are God's final warnings to humanity, calling them to repentance, but are not the final punishment. These disasters have not yet struck humanity; they only fell upon one third of the earth, leaving the remnant of humanity the opportunity to live and return to God.

Then comes the sound of the fifth trumpet, bringing tribulation on human beings themselves (cf. Rev. 9:4). Again, the goal of this tribulation is not to destroy human beings, but warn and awaken them in the hope that they may repent and return to God. Unfortunately, however, man will seek death instead of God, and annihilation instead of life (cf. Rev. 9:6).

When the sixth angel sounds the trumpet, the tribulation of man will become far more severe, so that perhaps man might wake up, forsake the worship of the idols he has fashioned for himself, and return to his God who made him (cf. Rev. 9:20–1). But again, unfortunately, these catastrophes will not cause man to awake, and he will persist in his transgression and his estrangement from God.

THE LAST TRUMPET

At the sound of the seventh trumpet, the Book of Revelation does not tell us about catastrophes that will occur, but of the fulfilment of God's promise to save His righteous servants (cf. Rev. 10:7). It does not mention what will happen on earth, but rather mentions the effect of these seven trumpets in heaven. There, we shall hear a hymn of joy and victory, because God and His Christ shall reign over all the kingdoms of the earth unto the age of ages:

> Then the seventh angel sounded: And there were loud voices in heaven, saying, 'The kingdoms of this world have become the kingdoms of our Lord and of His Christ, and He shall reign forever and ever!'. And the twenty-four elders who sat before God on their thrones fell on their faces and worshiped God, saying: 'We give You thanks, O Lord God Almighty, the One who is and who was and who is to come, because You have taken Your great power and reigned' (Rev. 11:15–18).

Secondly, the sound of the trumpet—as the Lord Jesus explained to His disciples—shall announce the coming of the Son of Man at the end of days, when He shall send out His angels with the great sound of a trumpet to gather His elect from one end of heaven to the other (Matt. 24:31). The phrase 'great sound of a trumpet' indicates that all the elect will hear it; that is, the Lord's coming will be made known to every human being on the face of the whole earth.

Lastly, the resurrection of the dead and the transformation that will befall the living will be completed at the sound of the last trumpet: 'in a moment, in the twinkling of an eye, at the last trumpet. For the trumpet will sound, and the dead will be raised incorruptible, and we shall be changed' (1 Cor. 15:52).

The last trumpet is not the last in a series of trumpets; it is last in the sense that there shall be no other trumpet after it; it is the last, and at its sounding the end will come:

> For the Lord Himself will descend from heaven with a shout, with the voice of an archangel, and with the trumpet of God. And the dead in Christ will rise first. Then we who are alive and remain shall be caught up together with them in the clouds to meet the Lord in the air. And thus we shall always be with the Lord (1 Thes. 4:16–17).

We feel that we are now at the end of days, where all the signs mentioned by the Lord as indications of the nearness of His coming are being fulfilled before our eyes every day. For this reason, we say with Paul the Apostle:

> …[you know] the time, that now it is high time to awake out of sleep; for now our salvation is nearer than when we first believed. The night is far spent, the day is at hand. Therefore let us cast off the works of darkness, and let us put on the armor of light (Rom. 13:11–12).

Let us be prepared to hear the sound of that last trumpet that every person will hear, either with sorrow or with joy: sorrow over the many warnings that passed without our awakening from sleep to repentance; or joy because our vessels are filled with oil, and our lamps burning in eager anticipation of the moment when we shall hear the trumpet calling us to gather together with the Lord:

> And thus we shall always be with the Lord. Therefore comfort one another with these words (1 Thes. 4:17–18).

APPENDIX:
SOME APOPHTHEGMS
OF OUR FATHER
BISHOP ANBA EPIPHANIUS

1. An Orthodox hegumenia[1] warmly greeted Anba Epiphanius and enthusiastically asked him about his community, 'At the Monastery of Saint Macarius you are many, aren't you? How many monks are there?'. Anba Epiphanius replied, 'Do you mean true monks or just "monks"? True monks are very few... as for "monks", they are about one hundred and forty.'

2. A brother asked him, 'How many priests are there at Saint Macarius?'. Anba Epiphanius replied, 'This question embarrasses me. They were few up until Fr. Matthew the Poor. Then fourteen were ordained together, and then twenty-eight. And now, even from the outside, other abbots are putting pressure on me to ordain the remaining monks. But I do not want that. With the novices who are about to be ordained monks I am very clear; I tell them, "If you want to be ordained priests, go elsewhere." I am convinced that what has ruined monasticism is money and clericalization. Can you imagine that one day one monk insisted so much that

---

[1] The mother in charge of a monastery of nuns.

he told me, "Either you ordain me a priest or I become a Muslim!"'.

3. Another brother asked the bishop, 'Are there always many pilgrims visiting the monastery?'. Anba Epiphanius replied, 'Yes, on some holidays there are very many.' The brother went on to ask what were the reasons that drove so many people to go to the monasteries. Anba Epiphanius replied, 'I respond in a way that applies to everyone. One day a family wakes up. Parents ask their children, "Where do you want to go? To the zoo or to the monastery?" The decision is put to the vote and the monastery wins. And the family finds itself in the monastery... If one goes to the monastery knowing where he goes, he receives blessings; otherwise, if he is not aware of it, it serves no purpose.'

4. A brother asked Anba Epiphanius to explain how candidates are trained for spiritual formation. Anba Epiphanius replied, 'When a young man approaches the monastery, he must attend for at least a year before entering, and he is looked after by the responsible for novices. Then upon entering, he receives the blue habit and spends another year. Then he receives another habit, a brown one, for another two years or so. And in the end, when he is ordained, we discover a completely different person from the one we had known!'.

5. A young man asked Anba Epiphanius what he thought about asceticism, self-purification, and self-control. Anba Epiphanius replied: 'A monk is one who forgets himself in order to unite with Christ. We must

forget ourselves in order to seek union with the Other. Asceticism and prayer are only means to reach deification.'

6. To another brother who asked him about personal prayer, he replied, 'Be constant in reciting the psalms in personal prayer. If you abandon them, it will be very difficult to go back to them again.'

7. Speaking about the monastic vocation, he added, 'The elders of the monastery said to me, "Do not enter again the house you came out from."'

8. Addressing the same young man, he explained, 'The first years for a monk are decisive. It is important to have a clear purpose. Father Matthew the Poor said that the first ten years for the monk are like the period of formation of the fetus in the womb. For the first ten years it is good to read only Scripture and monastic texts. Then read what you want.'

9. The same young man asked him what he thought about reading newspapers and magazines. Anba Epiphanius replied, 'When an elder of the monastery was brought newspapers from outside to be distributed among the monks, he replied, "Newspapers and magazines for the monks are like the grounding of an electrical system: they disperse their spiritual energy."'

10. Another brother asked him how at Saint Macarius they manage the use of mobile phones and the Internet. Anba Epiphanius replied: 'In the community, almost everyone now has a cell phone and Internet in his cell. Per se they are useful technologies, everything depends

on the use made of them. Browsing the Internet you can find books, just as you can look for something else...'.

11. A brother asked him how to become a hermit. Anba Epiphanius replied: 'In the old days it used to be that to become a hermit one needed the blessing of the whole community. Today, however, some decide on their own to become hermits, regardless of the community. But my experience tells me that only those who have lived well in community will live well as hermits. Those who have lived in the community the most, receive more blessings in solitude.'

12. In this regard he also said: 'In Oriental monasticism we only have the cell. In the West you have the blessing of doing something else for the brothers: there are the services imposed by common life; and if you want the cell you have that too.'

13. Concerning Western monasticism, he said: 'Western monasticism is very diverse compared to us Orientals. If one enters an oriental monastery, he does not know what he will do: he can remain a monk, he can become a priest and serve in a parish, he can become a bishop, and so on. In Western monasticism, the large number of monastic orders and congregations for religious life makes it possible to best express the vocation one feels within. If one seeks solitude, he finds it, if he seeks common life, he finds it, if he seeks teaching in schools, he finds it, if he seeks service in hospitals, he finds it, etc.'

14. Meeting the brothers at the table for Sunday lunch, Anba Epiphanius said that at Saint Macarius the monks meet on the Lord's Day to eat together. Towards the end of the meal, animated by a nice dialogue, he added: 'Nowadays at the table we read the Apophthegms of the Fathers, but anciently they talked and the young asked questions to the elders. It seems to me that I have returned to those times… but the elders are you.'

15. Repeatedly he said, taking up the saying of Abba Macarius, 'I have not yet become a monk myself, but I have seen monks!'.[2]

16. Once, to a novice who praised him, he replied with great courtesy but also firmly said: 'Listen, brother, you absolutely must learn a fundamental apophthegm for your monastic life: "Do not praise a monk in his face, otherwise you deliver him into the hands of the devil."'[3]

17. He also told a brother: 'If a brother makes a mistake and knows he was wrong, we must not treat him severely. Fr. Matthew the Poor taught us that the monks who make mistakes, even if they make serious mistakes, are the ones who need more love and acceptance. In order to repent and convert they must feel that they are loved. Even if you know his mistake, try not to reproach him but to treat him with mercy.'

---

[2] *Sayings of the Desert Fathers, Alphabetical collection*, Macarius, 2 (*Ward*: 125).

[3] *Sayings of the Desert Fathers, Systematic collection*, XXI, 54.

18. A brother asked him about some "disturbing" elements in the Monastery of Saint Macarius and then asked, 'What is patience?'. He replied, 'Patience is love. The Apostle says, in fact, that love is patient. God himself has an abundance of patience with us because He loves us. It is way too easy for me to expel those people who disturb, but then they will find themselves on the road. On the other hand, I hope that with patience and love, even if in ten years, they will convert.'

19. On the occasion of a meal together with Christians from different Churches not in communion with each other, while the discussion revolved around the deadlock at which the ecumenical dialogue arrived, Anba Epiphanius asked to be able to address a question to the diners: 'We now we are sitting here, all together, and we eat food that we all believe to have been sanctified by our common prayer. I wonder then: what prevents us from communicating together to the Body and Blood of Christ?'.

20. Repeatedly he said the following saying of St Pachomius: 'It is said of Saint Pachomius that he was once working with his brothers and that this work required that each of them carry a large quantity of bread. One of the young men said to him: "Never let it be that you bring something, Father. Behold, I bring what is enough for me and for you together." The saint replied: "Never let this be. If it has been written of the Lord that He wanted to resemble His brothers in everything (cf. Heb 2:17), how could I, the ignoble, distinguish myself

from my brothers so as not to carry my burden like them."[4]

21. Repeatedly he told the saying of Abba Zacharias: 'One day Abba Moses said to brother Zacharias, "Tell me what I ought to do?" At these words the latter threw himself on the ground at the old man's feet and said, "Are you asking me, Father?" The old man said to him, "Believe me, Zacharias, my son, I have seen the Holy Spirit descending upon you and since then I am constrained to ask you." Then Zacharias drew his hood off his head put it under his feet and trampled on it, saying, "The man who does not let himself be treated thus, cannot become a monk."'[5]

22. To some of us, he said, 'I cannot prevent any Christian from taking communion who believes that what I have in my hands is the Body and Blood of Christ.'

23. At the end of his speech at the Conference on Orthodox Spirituality, to those who asked him for his opinion about the division between Christians, he said, 'Forgive me, I am not a theologian. I do not understand divisions. I only know what unity is.'

24. Then, personally, to a young brother who was still questioning him about this, he said: 'In ecumenical dialogues we cannot expect to come to think of it all in the same way. It is necessary to distinguish between

---

[4] *Apophthegm* 75, in *Bustān* (48).
[5] *Sayings of the Desert Fathers, Alphabetical collection*, Zacharia, 3 (*Ward*: 68).

dogma and theological opinion. I mean, do we all believe in the Trinity? Well! Then if I interpret the Trinity in one way and the other in another it can be the object of dialogue, but it cannot prevent us from being united. We are talking about theological hypotheses. The Fathers of the Church themselves diverged on this point. I will give you another example. There is the case, at the beginning of Christianity, of two heresies: a heresy believed in the Trinity and another did not. One baptized in the name of the Trinity, the other in the name of Jesus. At Nicaea the baptism of the first was accepted because it was conferred in the name of the Trinity, despite being heretical on other issues.' The brother replied: 'Yes, but how do you see the question of the infallibility of the Church? For us Catholics, for example, it is clear that the Council of Vatican I is a problem, and yet no one will ever dream of openly admitting that at that juncture the Church gathered in council confused the truth with error.' Anba Epiphanius replied: 'Yet the Church can make mistakes. The great problem faced by the Churches today is the ecclesial ego. The last Catholic popes have made a very important gesture by asking for forgiveness. And asking for forgiveness is admitting that you were wrong, and therefore recognizing the fallibility of the Church. Furthermore, we must always ask ourselves what we are looking for. Are we really looking for unity or not? You know well that it is even possible to make the Bible say something and its exact opposite. Everything depends on what we are looking for. The same applies to the statements of the Church. If we truly want unity, we will find words of unity, and everything else will take a second place.'

25. When asked what he thought of Pope Francis, Anba Epiphanius replied: 'Pope Francis is a spiritual man. When there is a spiritual leader at the head of the Church, the whole Church is brought up. Not so when an intellectual is there. And I say this as one who has always loved studying myself: being intellectual is not enough. It is the spiritual person that brings people closer to God.'

26. He said again: 'Here there are people, who are not officially in communion, who call the others 'brothers and sisters' from the tribune. What brotherhood do they mean? If they mean the one inaugurated by Christ and do not seriously seek the unity of the Body of the Church, then they are liars!'.